Step 1:   We admitted we were powerless over our dependency and that our lives had become   unmanageable.

Because of the extravagance of those revelations, and so I wouldn't get a big head, I was given the gift of a handicap to keep me in constant touch with my limitations. Satan's angel did his best to get me down; what he in fact did was push me to my knees. No danger then of walking around high and mighty! At first I didn't think of it as a gift, and begged God to remove it. Three times I did that, and then he told me, My grace is enough; it's all you need. My strength comes into its own in your weakness. Once I heard that, I was glad to let it happen. I quit focusing on the handicap and began appreciating the gift. It was a case of Christ's strength moving in on my weakness. Now I take limitations in stride, and with good cheer, these limitations that cut me down to size—abuse, accidents, opposition, bad breaks. I just let Christ take over! And so the weaker I get, the stronger I become.

2 Corinthians 12:7-10 The Message

National Association for Christian Recovery
563 Southlake Blvd.
Richmond, VA 23235
info@nacr.org

Published through Kindle Direct Publishing @ kdp.amazon.com

Interior design: Jessica Faillace

ISBN: 9781080975563

STEP 1: WE ADMITTED WE WERE POWERLESS OVER OUR DEPENDENCIES AND THAT OUR LIVES WERE UNMANAGEABLE.

Table of Contents

Step 1: We admitted we were powerless over our dependencies and that our lives were unmanageable.

Introduction

I co-pastor a recovery church and serve as the Executive Director of the National Association for Christian Recovery. My work grants me access to amazing stories of hope from people who have utilized the 12-Step process to heal and restore their lives. I practice these steps myself and know first-hand how frustrating, freeing and practical this work is as a daily discipline. I have learned that my problems, my personality and even my preferences are not fixed in stone. We are all far more interesting and complicated than labels and "isms". The Steps are a tool that helps us acknowledge truth while gently and persistently guiding us back home to God and our most true selves. I did not grow up in a home that practiced religion of any sort. I was unaware that I needed to wrestle with God or surrender to his will. What I did know was that I was lonely, angry, tired and hungry - hungry for SOMETHING that would satisfy my soul. The steps guided me on a spiritual pilgrimage that has been healing and transformative for me.

This study is intended to provide an opportunity for participants to consider both their recovery and their spirituality as two sides of the same coin. I experience the Twelve Steps as a spiritual program that fits seamlessly into a Christian framework, which happens to be the lens I look through in my search for God. AA, for various valid reasons, is not explicitly created for a Christian audience; this material seeks to include a Christian perspective for folks who are interested in working a 12-step program with more explicit Christian commentary. Along the way, there will be times when the language of recovery or the language of faith causes us discomfort. When this happens speak up and ask for clarification! There is no need to make this work harder than it needs to be simply because we had a misunderstanding of terminology! In particular, we have learned over the years how shaming and judgmental words like "alcoholic" and "addict" can be for folks. In an effort to reduce stigma, today's preferred terminology is "substance use disorder". This is helpful because it is more accurate - it indicates that this malady is on a spectrum and provides a framework consistent with observations about the disease. That said, some of my friends in recovery have worked long and hard to come to acceptance of their disease. They cannot get on board with this new lingo. It is part of their work to specifically name their disorder - "alcoholic", "addict", etc. In this material we will use substance use disorder (SUD) AND sometimes for brevity's sake we will use or quote others who use the older terminology. Wherever you land in the discussion, it might be helpful to think of the issue like this: *There may be adjectives that I can use to describe myself that are inappropriate or unadvisable for you to use to describe me. SUDers may find using more specific labels helpful; the rest of us show more respect to others when we use less stigmatizing language.* My prayer is that this journey will bring you peace, healing and a love for yourself, God and others that is beyond your wildest dreams. I pray that God will give you understanding, a willingness to both pursue him and receive him as he pursues you. I pray that you will be given the strength to carry out his will for you. And in some small way, I hope this study guide is a blessing to you as you walk your path.

Blessings, Teresa McBean

(You can contact Teresa via her email: teresa@nacr.org)

STEP 1: WE ADMITTED WE WERE POWERLESS OVER OUR DEPENDENCIES AND THAT OUR LIVES WERE UNMANAGEABLE.

Suggestions for Using this Guide

This is your work; please use this guide any way it serves you! In the meeting rooms, participants are encouraged to "take what works and leave the rest". Good advice for this material as well! Each study has the following elements:

Moment by Moment - Meditation

Brief suggestions for how to begin each study with a meditation. A variety of ways to meditate are explored. Meditation speeds the recovery process, is good for healing our brain (which is compromised in SUD), and is a tool that will be helpful in maintaining long term sobriety. Among other benefits, it lowers blood pressure, reduces stress, mitigates anxiety and can increase our conscious contact with God. (**Appendix A** provides helpful hints, articles and more detailed suggestions for meditation.)

Prayer for the moment

Excerpts from Dale and Juanita's book **Rooted in God's Love**. The Ryans' wrote their devotional book in response to their own experience with recovery. This section includes a scripture passage, brief words on the subject and a closing prayer. It is a way to center in and begin to focus on the spirituality of the step.

Thoughts for the Day and By the Book[1]

Story is healing; sharing our experience, strength and hope is crucial to recovery. This section is about the author's experience with recovery – from the perspectives of both her own issues and as a family member of a sufferer as well as her decades of experience in recovery ministry. Sprinkled throughout the material are quotes from a video series of men and women sharing their experience with the Twelve Steps.

Consider Your Story:

Connecting with the prompts that may arise through prayer, meditation and engaging with the stories about substance use disorder, each study provides a few questions to prompt the reader to explore their own story of recovery. Although space is provided in the workbook for responding, you may want to add a journal or notebook to capture more detailed responses or further journal about your experience.

After you complete Step 1, our Step 2 workbook awaits you!

---

[1] Video sources for **By the Book** can be found by going to:
https://www.nacr.org/center-for-12-step-recovery/by-the-book-doing-the-twelve-steps

Step 1: *We admitted we were powerless over our dependencies and that our lives were unmanageable.*

Study #1 - Step 1

Moment by Moment - Meditation

Breathe. In and out. Count your breaths. When you find yourself distracted with thoughts and worries, start over with "one" and keep counting.

Prayer for the Moment[2]

I pray that you, being rooted and established in love may have power...to grasp...the love of Christ.
Ephesians 3:17-18

We all have root systems. Roots are life-lines. They seek out and drink in water and nutrients. And they provide stability in times of wind and erosion.

Unfortunately, many of us are rooted in the soil of shame. Roots in this rocky soil become bound. They cannot sustain growth. They are not able to provide nourishment or stability.

Recovery for many of us is like being transplanted. It is the process of allowing God to first pull us out of the parched and rocky soil of shame and to then plant us in the soil of love. In the rich soil of love our fragile roots can finally begin to stretch, grow and take hold. It is a soil in which real nourishment and real stability are possible.

But transplantation is not a simple matter. No matter how gently God pulls us up out of the soil of shame, there will be distress. And sinking roots in new soil will feel like an unfamiliar and risky adventure.

As our roots sink deeper and deeper in the soil of God's love, however, we will begin to experience growth that never could have been possible in the soil of rejection and shame. We will become "rooted and established" in love.

---

[2] Prayers for the moment are excerpted with permission from *Rooted in God's Love, Meditations on Biblical Texts for People in Recovery* by Dale and Juanita Ryan, 2005, pp. 14-15.

STEP 1: WE ADMITTED WE WERE POWERLESS OVER OUR DEPENDENCIES AND THAT OUR LIVES WERE UNMANAGEABLE.

My roots are in poor soil, Lord.
They do not nourish.
They provide no stability.
My roots are bound, Lord.
Transplant me.
Give me grace-full soil, Lord.
Sink my roots deeply.
Give me stability.
Nourish me
in your love.

Amen

Additional Prayers:

Thoughts for the Day

Thirty-three years ago my brother acknowledged his addictions and entered a treatment facility in Atlanta, Georgia. It was mid-January, cold, with a steady downfall of sleet turning the streets into an ice rink – never a good look for the south. Decades later, no one can explain how he remembered the number of our oldest brother (from whom he was estranged), managed to find the humility and desperation to call and ask for help or perhaps the greatest mystery of all – why he thought anyone in our family would be willing to risk their own neck to go save his sorry you-know-what after "all he had put us through". But call he did and that initiated a cascading response of help from a family that, like many families in the throes of Substance Use Disorder, were sick and tired of being sick and tired.

> "I think...the first step is not about 'we admitted we are powerless over alcohol and our lives had become unmanageable', meaning life isn't manageable because I am powerless over alcohol. The deeper meaning of that statement is my LIFE is unmanageable and I drink alcohol as a way of dealing with that; it is a symptom of the unmanageability.[3]
>
> By the Book

In the time it took my heroic brother to drive from north Atlanta to midtown in the wee hours of the morning my substance abusing brother lost his moment of clarity. But one brother did not risk his own life and limb for the other only to give up and go home just because a very sick young man changed his mind. Through persuasion and coercion, phone calls, threats and a frantic search for in-patient treatment options within driving distance, we found a facility that would take my brother. Next, we needed to find a large sum of money. A request for this ridiculously large check was made to our parents through a strikingly similar set of conversations requiring persuasion, coercion and shaming. Off to treatment he went. His sobriety date is January 21, 1986. Slowly, painstakingly, our family entered recovery that is best measured in decades not days, with mixed results which have included both transformation and tragedy. Recovery wrecked and restored parts of our family. Nothing about this process has been easy, but the most difficult part of all was admitting our powerlessness. This turned out to be a somewhat collective admission for our family with varying degrees of honesty and recovery work. Certainly, that first call started the snowball rolling. Oftentimes the first step feels like a long walk off a short pier in total isolation. Like most things in recovery, our first instincts are often misguided.

Two are better than one, because they have a good return for their work: if one falls down, his friend can help him up. But pity the man who falls and has no one to help him up!
Eccl. 4:9, 10 NIV

---

[3] *https://www.nacr.org/center-for-12-step-recovery/by-the-book-doing-the-twelve-steps/by-the-book-step-1* at 17:30.

Consider Your Story

How does this story remind you of your own? Journal about your own story.

Who do you most relate to in the story? Explain.

Study #2 - Step 1

Moment by Moment - Meditation

Sit with your feet on the floor. Roll your shoulders back; try to sit in both an alert and reasonably comfortable position. Breathe. In and out. Count your breaths.

Prayer for the Moment[4]

Suppose one of you has a hundred sheep and loses one of them. Does he not leave the ninety-nine in the open country and go after the lost sheep until he finds it? And when he finds it, he joyfully puts it on his shoulders and goes home. Then he calls his friends and neighbors together and says, 'Rejoice with me; I have found my lost sheep.'
Luke 15:4-5 NIV

It is easy for us to lose our way. We may start off with confidence. We think we know where we are and where we are headed. And, then, somewhere along the way in life we get lost. We find ourselves alone and we don't know where we are. We get confused and disoriented. We don't know how to find our way back, how to get "on track" again. Fortunately, God pays attention. God notices that we are lost. And, because of the great value God sees in us, God sets out to find us. God searches for us. God pursues us until we are found.

When God finds us, most of us expect God to say: "Where have you been? I have been looking all over for you? I don't want to have to come back out here again to find you." But there is no hint of scolding, shaming, yelling, or blaming in this text. When God finds us, God is full of joy. God picks us up and carries us home. God celebrates.

God pays attention, notices when we are lost, searches for us, and celebrates when we are found. Recovery is the gift of being found by God.

---

[4] Prayers for the moment are excerpted with permission from *Rooted in God's Love, Meditations on Biblical Texts for People in Recovery* by Dale and Juanita Ryan, 2005, pp. 16-17.

I was lost, Lord.
Alone. Disoriented. Confused. Afraid.
You found me.
I expected blame and rejection when you found me.
I expected you to be full of rage.
I expected you to see me as an inconvenience.
But you greeted me with joy.
With celebration!
Thank you for finding me.
Thank you for carrying me home with joy.

Amen

Additional Prayers:

Step 1: We admitted we were powerless over our dependencies and that our lives were unmanageable.

Thoughts for the Day

My people are broken—shattered!—and they put on Band-Aids, saying, 'It's not so bad. You'll be just fine.' But things are not 'just fine'!

Jeremiah 6:14 The Message

My brother's substance use disorder was as simple and as complicated as anyone else's story who struggles with this disease. Our understanding of it as a family has shifted over the years, often in sync with our collective cultural awakening to the nature of the affliction.

James Morrison wrote a book, **DSM-5 Made Easy,** *The Clinician's Guide to Diagnosis*[5]. (The DSM-5 is shorthand for the book **The Diagnostic and Statistical Manual of Mental Disorders.**) Families are not the only ones who struggle to understand this baffling disease. Clinicians and researchers have fretted over the definition of addiction for decades. (More detailed quotes on the subject from Dr. Morrison can be found in **Appendix B.**) In summary, it seems everyone can agree that whatever we "use" compulsively eventually turns on us; it never delivers on its promise to make us feel "normal" or "happy" or "capable". This is the human condition – we search for shortcuts that we hope will fulfill us. But not all of us end up with a substance use disorder. Why does this happen to some and not others? No one has all the answers to this question. This affliction is physiological, mental, emotional and spiritual in nature. All elements of our body, mind and spirit are impacted by the disorder. Use ends up causing distress and additional problems. Whether our "ism" is alcohol, drugs, shopping, sex, eating or not eating, gambling, etc., eventually our dependency on this "thing" interferes with our daily lives. According to Dr. Morrison, there are five essential features that are present with substance abuse that cause chronic or repeated problems. They are:

1. Personal and interpersonal life
2. Employment
3. Control
4. Health and safety
5. Physiological sequels - meaning, tolerance develops and withdrawal occurs with disuse.

> "It is the natural state of the alcoholic, the only relief [we] know is through drugs and alcohol...[we] totally lack coping skills."[6]
>
> By The Book

---

[5] James Morrison, *DSM-5 Made Easy, The Clinician's Guide to Diagnosis,* (The Guilford Press, 72 Spring Street, New York, NY 10012, 2014), p. 398.
[6] *https://www.nacr.org/center-for-12-step-recovery/by-the-book-doing-the-twelve-steps/by-the-book-step-1* at 17:30.

Consider Your Story

Refer back to Dr. Morrison's 5 Essential Features of Substance Abuse. Any health problems, disabilities, failures at work, school or home that have caused you pain and suffering? List them.

What are your recurring worries/fears? (Like job, family issues, money, God, sex, legal issues)

Study #3 - Step 1

Moment by Moment - Meditation

Sit with your feet on the floor. Roll your shoulders back; try to sit in both an alert and reasonably comfortable position. Breathe. In and out. Breathe deeply, all the way into your belly, release your breath slowly but fully. Count your breaths. When you find yourself distracted with thoughts and worries, start over with one and keep counting until you need to restart. See if you can make it to twenty breaths without distractions. But if you only make it to ten, that's ok. When you get antsy, stop.

Prayer for the Moment[7]

> *I have stilled and quieted my soul; like a weaned child with its mother,*
> *Like a weaned child is my soul within me.*
> *Psalm 131:2*

A weaned child in the psalmist's culture is a child who can walk and talk. It is a child who for many months has been nourished day and night at its mother's breast. Every time the pain of hunger came, the child enjoyed the powerful combination of having its stomach filled with warm milk while being held in a close, intimate embrace. Messages of love and valuing flowed into the child's spirit while the life-sustaining milk flowed into its body.

Love and nourishment are the soil in which security grows. Weaned children still need to eat, but they are not frantic about their next meal. Weaned children have learned that their needs are important, that they will be noticed and that their needs will be met. As a result, they have grown secure.

Recovery is like being loved and nourished until we can be weaned. We don't grow out of having needs. But as we experience love and nourishment, we gradually become less frantic about our next meal. We grow. We heal. Eventually a new kind of security grows in us - not the security of toxic self-reliance, but the security that comes from nurture. We become less frantic, less fragile. Our souls become stilled and quieted.

---

[7] Prayers for the moment are excerpted with permission from *Rooted in God's Love, Meditations on Biblical Texts for People in Recovery* by Dale and Juanita Ryan, 2005, pp. 18-19.

Step 1: We admitted we were powerless over our dependencies and that our lives were unmanageable.

Nourish me, Lord.
Nourish me with your love.
Calm the frantic feelings within me.
Grow a sense of security within me.
I want to be able to sit quietly.
Like a weaned child.
Nourished.
Secure in your love.

Amen

Additional Prayers:

Thoughts for the Day

A dependency, compulsion, urge - whatever you call it, is a coping strategy that we use in excess to solve a problem. Maybe it relieves anxiety or depression, sometimes it helps us feel normal or more sociable. We are in "excess" when our behaviors begin to have consequences. Compulsions of all sorts share this one true thing: **"excess" disrupts lives**. My brother's cocaine addiction, unlike my own eating disorder, caused him to break out in handcuffs, lose jobs and generally manage to infuriate anyone who tried to maintain a relationship with him. He lied, he cheated, he stole. I lied in ways that were equally damaging but a teeny tiny bit less obvious than his dramatic crash and burns. In fact, his own propensity to get into massive amounts of trouble served to mask the dysfunction of our family system in general and in particular our individual issues. He was the black sheep, providing a welcome distraction from the truth - we were all like sheep who had gone astray. Some might say that we had wandered far from God; but the truth is we hadn't really wandered so much as we never even considered ourselves in relationship to a Higher Power.

The crisis created by my brother's treatment for drug addiction provided an opportunity for our family to take time to assess the dynamics at play in our family system. Problems that seemed obvious to others were revelations to us. Secrets were exposed. My eating disorder was named. The rigid roles that each family member played: the enabling, the lying, a lot of these realities rose to our collective consciousness. (Again, this was not everyone's perspective.) Suddenly, what we thought of as 'normal' shifted. We realized how unmanageable our lives were - the conflicts, the financial strain of dealing with my brother's issues, the unhealthy ways my parents coped with their stress, the resentments we held against one another but never discussed. We learned that much of this was related to the disease of addiction. It was a multi-generational problem. Both the affliction and maladaptive coping skills associated with addiction were passed down through our family tree much like the family silver and a few pieces of good jewelry. When we take our first step the focus rightfully belongs on our own particular brand of compulsivity. But it is also helpful to realize that when one family member suffers from substance use disorder, the entire family system is also suffering various forms of sickness marked by denial, unmanageability, powerlessness and resistance to solving problems.

But I need something more! For if I know the law but still can't keep it, and if the power of sin within me keeps sabotaging my best intentions, I obviously need help! I realize that I don't have what it takes. I can will it, but I can't do it. I decide to do good, but I don't really do it; I decide not to do bad, but then I do it anyway. My decisions, such as they are, don't result in actions. Something has gone wrong deep within me and gets the better of me every time.
Romans 7:17-20 The Message

STEP 1: WE ADMITTED WE WERE POWERLESS OVER OUR DEPENDENCIES AND THAT OUR LIVES WERE UNMANAGEABLE.

Consider Your Story

Upon reflection, what kind of compulsions and dependencies have you noticed in your own family?

What dependencies and/or compulsions do you practice to cope with life?

What is it that you think you NEED help with?

Step 1: We admitted we were powerless over our dependencies and that our lives were unmanageable.

Study #4 - Step 1

Moment by Moment - Meditation

Sit with your feet on the floor. Roll your shoulders back; try to sit in both an alert and reasonably comfortable position. Breathe. In and out. Count your breaths. When you find yourself distracted with thoughts and worries, start over with one and keep counting until you need to restart.

Prayer for the Moment[8]

Then we will no longer be infants, tossed back and forth by the waves, and blown here and there by every wind of teaching and by the cunning and craftiness of men in their deceitful scheming. Instead, speaking the truth in love, we will in all things grow up into him who is the Head, that is, Christ. From him the whole body, joined and held together by every supporting ligament, grows and builds itself up in love, as each part does its work.

Ephesians 4:14-16

Why can't you grow up?! Parents sometimes express their anger and impatience with their children in this way. But, it is not a shameful thing to be a child. To acknowledge our child-like-ness is to acknowledge our limits and our dependency. It is to make room for wonder, trust and joy in our lives. It is to be curious, spontaneous and playful. If that is what it means to be a child, then we need more of it.

But there is also a sense, as in this text, in which to be childlike is to be immature or unstable. It is a good thing to grow-up. Not because it is shameful to be a child, but because growth is part of God's plan for us. Being "tossed back and forth" is an exhausting way to live. We need to find some way to live without being "blown here and there".

Growing up is hard work. The reason for this, as this text suggests, is that growing up is closely connected with learning to speak the truth in love. Honesty is a central dynamic of growth and recovery. Increasing our capacity for honesty is not an easy process. But as we speak the truth in love, we will experience some dramatic changes in our relationships. We will know what it is to be secure in God's love - clear about the truth of God's love for us. We will find a more intimate relationship with God - we will "grow up into Christ".

---

[8] Prayers for the moment are excerpted with permission from *Rooted in God's Love, Meditations on Biblical Texts for People in Recovery* by Dale and Juanita Ryan, 2005, pp. 20-21.

Help me to be a child, Lord.
Help me to face my needs and my limits.
Free me to enjoy the trust and wonder and joy of a child.
But, help me to grow up well.
I'm tired of being tossed back and forth.
I want more stability than being blown here and there.
I want to have stable, healthy relationships with you, and with others.
So, build within me a capacity for honesty.
Help me to speak the truth in love so that I can grow up.
Cause me to grow into a strong sheltering tree
planted securely in the truth of your love.

Amen

Additional Prayers:

STEP 1: WE ADMITTED WE WERE POWERLESS OVER OUR DEPENDENCIES AND THAT OUR LIVES WERE UNMANAGEABLE.

Thoughts for the Day

Is substance use disorder a moral failure? Some treat it as such. Is diabetes a moral failure? What about cancer? What about strep throat?

"God has turned his back on me," says a young man lying on a gurney in the Emergency Room.

"Tell me more about that," I reply.

"Man, you know it's true." His raised voice attracts the attention of the on-duty nurse and she peeks around the curtain with eyebrows raised but I wave her off. This young man has something to say and I am here to listen. "I'm a loser. Even my own grandmother won't let me visit anymore. I'm a drug addict. I'm weak. I'm a disappointment to everyone who ever loved me." He turns his head away from me and stares blankly at the wall, slipping off into an exhausted slumber. He has been on the street for months; he is feeling ashamed and embarrassed. He is without hope and expects no help. He and his family believe that he is spiritually and morally bankrupt. This would not be the case if he had been diagnosed with cancer, diabetes, or strep throat. I look at him and believe that he has a disease that has had physical, relational, emotional and spiritual consequences. Obviously, a by-product of compulsions that turn into addictions involves the inevitable self-destructive behaviors that result in desperate choices that are hurtful. When grandma's flat screen television gets stolen in order to feed an addiction, this falls under the category of the sin of "do not steal" - not to mention the unwritten law of "Always love your grandma because she gives you cookies for breakfast!" But this is not the whole story.

If we try to understand our substance use disorder only as SIN, as if that explains everything and points to the obvious and only solution of REPENTANCE - we are speaking out of ignorance and reflect an inadequate understanding of the nature of the disease. Substance use disorder hijacks the brain and robs us of the capacity to experience love and connection with God, ourselves and others. Despite what many believe, substance use disordered folks are not people who just need to know Jesus and pray with more fervor. Many have had profound spiritual experiences, believe in God, have even served him in various capacities before this affliction robbed them of their sense of self-respect (among other things). Not all folks who struggle with SUD have spiritual backgrounds, but many do AND IT DID NOT PROTECT THEM FROM THIS AFFLICTION ANY MORE THAN IT PROTECTS US FROM CANCER. Those of us who suffer with SUD have lost touch with ourselves and our values. But our "sin" is not the cause of our SUD, it is part of our humanity. All of us forget God and ourselves and even lose our way, whether or not we have a SUD.

You can't whitewash your sins and get by with it; you find mercy by admitting and leaving them.
Proverbs 28:13 The Message

STEP 1: WE ADMITTED WE WERE POWERLESS OVER OUR DEPENDENCIES AND THAT OUR LIVES WERE UNMANAGEABLE.

Consider Your Story

What do you feel guilt or shame about?

What are your thoughts on "sin" and its role in your addiction?

How does thinking about addiction as having both a genetic and physiological component impact your self-assessment?

How would you and your family approach your recovery differently if everyone understood that there is a physiological component to your Substance Use Disorder?

Step 1: We admitted we were powerless over our dependencies and that our lives were unmanageable.

Study #5 - Step 1

Moment by Moment - Meditation

Take a few moments to sit and breathe. Count your breaths. Notice the tension in your body. As you breathe, concentrate on directing your breath to the tension. Common tense spots include: the jaw, back, shoulders, rib cage and gut. Breathe. Start at your head and observe your body. Intentionally try to relax each body part from top to bottom while maintaining good posture. After your body scan, take three deep cleansing breaths and slowly open your eyes.

Prayer for the Moment[9]

Not that I have already obtained all this, or have already been made perfect, but I press on to take hold of that for which Christ Jesus took hold of me.
Philippians 3:12

Some days the desire to be "finished" with recovery is almost overwhelming. It is such an attractive thought. To be done. It sounds so good. Done. Finally. Please, Lord, I want to be finished with my recovery today.

But we have learned something about our capacity for self-deceit. We have learned that we are not entirely in control of the process of recovery. And we have learned something about the dangers of complacency. It can lead us back into denial - and toward relapse. There is no more dangerous moment for us than the moment we become convinced that we are all better.

Recovery is "pressing on". We have not "already obtained". We have not "already been made perfect". Tomorrow's recovery cannot be done in advance. And yesterday's recovery, although it has changed and enriched us, is not the same thing as today's recovery. Today's recovery can only be done today.

The process of recovery restructures our lives in some very fundamental ways. We had learned silence, and in recovery we learn to speak the truth. We had learned not to feel, and in recovery we learn to feel. We had learned either not to need other people at all or to be excessively dependent on other people, and in recovery we learn to need other people in healthy ways. These are significant changes. But they are not irreversible changes. We can go back to silence, emotional numbness and unhealthy relationships. Recovery is necessarily therefore a new way of life. It is a daily pressing on. It is the day-at-a-time practice of the disciplines of recovery that makes it possible for us to continue to heal, grow and change.

---

[9] Prayers for the moment are excerpted with permission from *Rooted in God's Love, Meditations on Biblical Texts for People in Recovery* by Dale and Juanita Ryan, pp. 22- 23.

Lord, you have brought me so far.
Thank you.
I am grateful for all I have gained.
But, I want to press on.
I want to continue to grow.
I want to continue to learn.
Help me to press on.
Help me to do today's recovery today.
Help me to press on toward you.
Take hold of me with your love.

Amen

P.S. When I started recovery from my eating disorder, I did NOT want to press on. But I did want to get out from under the oppression of my disease. If this prayer doesn't resonate with you - no worries. Sometimes, as they say in the meeting rooms, we have to "fake it 'til we make it." I am not, as a general rule, a fan of faking stuff. But sometimes we have to pray for the healing thing, even if our body, mind, and spirit rebel at the thought of the healing. When I prayed at the beginning of my journey, I imagined myself running from a giant bear, fighting for my life. I was in survival mode. I prayed as a cry of desperation, not a prayer of hope. If this is your situation, perhaps my imagination will help you prayer without feeling like a fake!

Additional Prayers:

Step 1: We admitted we were powerless over our dependencies and that our lives were unmanageable.

Thoughts for the Day

How do we make sense of the language of "sin" as it relates to addiction? If substance use disorder can be compared to diabetes, where does the concept of "sin" fit in? Elbert Hubbard (not to be confused with L. Ron Hubbard) wrote, **"We are punished by our sins not for them."**[10] Claudio Naranjo, a Chilean-born psychiatrist, was known for integrating psychotherapy and the spiritual traditions in his work. **He talks about sin as it relates to ignorance, difficulties, distresses and embarrassments as "a disorder of awareness and an interference with action."**[11]

Substance use disorder is disorienting; we lose our way; we lose the essence of who we were created to be - beloved children, made in the image of God. Think about the scriptures we have considered in this material thus far - recovery that heals is rooted in love, in particular - God's love. God chases us down, not to berate us but to restore us, in love. Recovery is an opportunity to increase our capacity for honesty. Do these concepts sound like God is more concerned with our "sin" or our restoration?

The "s" word - sin - is a double-edged sword. When I do something wrong the healthy response is guilt. If I am not disoriented, ignorant, or embarrassed, I know how to respond. I admit I am wrong; I make amends; I do the appropriate work of restoration. To the extent that self-awareness of wrongdoing helps us repair the mess we made of things, it is a useful construct.

Personally, I often feel a lot of shame when I think of my behavior as "sinful". This shame-filled reaction stymied my recovery. Shame is never helpful - it encourages hiding, lying and defensiveness. Shame adds fuel to the fire of our feelings of despair and unworthiness. Shame may cause us to lose touch with our spirituality, our true purpose for living, and our capacity to live comfortably in community with others. Part of recovery that I benefited from the most was learning how to distinguish between productive guilt and toxic shame. We can learn how to reject shame and embrace guilt as an indicator that guides our next right steps.

This is not to diminish the role of "sin" in our lives; thinking of sin in the way that the above authors suggest can actually deepen our capacity to reckon with it through the lens of compassion. It invites each of us to nonjudgmentally observe ourselves and get honest about our issues. It helps us understand that "sin" is a by-product of our humanity, not a condemnation of our personhood.

... whatever overpowers you, enslaves you.
2 Peter 2:19 (b) CEB

---

[10] *The Note Book of Elbert Hubbard: Mottoes, Epigrams, Short Essay, Passages, Orphic Sayings and Preachments* (New York: Wm. B. Wise & CO1., 1927), p. 12.

[11] Claudio Naranjo, *The Enneagram of Society: Healing the Soul to healing the World* (Nevada City, CA: Gateways Books and Tapes, 2004), p. 22.

Consider Your Story

Make a list of the behaviors that your or someone you love has labeled as "sinful" in your life.

Think about the idea of being punished "by" rather than "for" those "sins". What changes for you? Does it change how you think about yourself, others, God and your SUD? Journal about this.

Study #6 - Step 1

Moment by Moment - Meditation

Go for a walk. Walk mindfully. Pay attention to your feet hitting the ground, notice the world around you. Listen to your breathing. Notice colors, sounds, smells. Walk leisurely. When you find your mind wandering, take a deep breath to reset, pause for a few beats, and then continue your stroll.

Prayer for the Moment[12]

Then they cried to the Lord in their trouble, and he saved them from their distress. He brought them out of darkness and the deepest gloom and broke away their chains. Let them give thanks to the Lord for his unfailing love and his wonderful deeds for men, for he breaks down gates of bronze and cuts through bars of iron.

Psalm 107:13-16

Addictions and compulsions are a kind of bondage. Painful memories are also like chains that bind us. We try harder and harder to change. But sometimes the harder we try, the tighter the chains become. Recovery begins when we recognize that our bondage is too great for us. We are not powerful enough to break these chains. Either we will find a power greater than ourselves to help us, or we will stay in bondage.

Many people find the idea of powerlessness troubling. We want to be competent and self-reliant. And, many of us have had people attempt to "rescue" us in ways that have increased our shame and self-contempt. So, why should we welcome the God-who-rescues? Won't God also shame us?

First, notice in this text that God's intervention is in response to a request. We do not serve a codependent God. God is not entangled in our compulsions. God will not rescue in ways that are shame-full. God knows that we need to be ready to be helped and that we need to cry out for help.

Notice also in this text that it is the God-of-unfailing-love who is our higher power. Because so many of us are convinced that God is vindictive, punitive and abusive, it can be terrifying in our powerlessness to focus on the power of God. We are sure that all of that power will be used against us. But the God-of-unfailing-love is not a vindictive, punitive or abusive God. God is a God-of-tough-love. That's the only kind of love that can be "unfailing." But God is not *against* us. God is *for* us.

Recovery is being set free by God's powerful love.

---

[12] Prayers for the moment are excerpted with permission from *Rooted in God's Love, Meditations on Biblical Texts for People in Recovery* by Dale and Juanita Ryan, 2005, pp. 24-25.

Step 1: We admitted we were powerless over our dependencies and that our lives were unmanageable.

I was powerless, Lord.
I expected you to increase my shame and self-contempt.
But you are a God of unfailing love.
I expected you to use your power against me.
But when I called, you came.
You crashed the gates.
You cut the bars.
You broke the chains.
You are leading me out of this darkness
and deepest gloom
into the light of day.
Thank you.

Amen

Additional Prayers:

Thoughts for the Day

Once, a long time ago, a friend of mine valiantly tried to convince me that I was starving myself to death. I was having none of it. I was not quite ready to admit that my eating was beyond weird and had moved from bad habits that I acted on compulsively into a substance use disorder. I was using the chemicals that my brain produced when I was in starvation mode to comfort myself and distract me from the deeper issues that were causing me great suffering.

My life was out of control. Today, I can admit that I knew something was wrong; I can tell the truth about the shame I felt about my body and my starvation diet. Shame plagued me, dominating my thoughts. It berated me, insisting that I was without value unless I was super skinny, practically perfect and pleasing to all.

Shame is the emotion that tells me that I am broken beyond repair. Shame is not guilt. Guilt is an emotional acknowledgement that I have done a particular thing wrong. It is circumstance specific. Shame is all-pervasive; shame lies and tells me that I am UNIQUELY AND TERMINALLY FLAWED.

Back then? I was withdrawn, defensive and arrogant. I believed that people who ate three meals a day were weak-willed, even disgusting. This is part of what a substance use disorder costs us. It robs us of our ability to love ourselves, God and others. I was also filled with self-loathing. It's a Jedi mind trick to be both arrogant and filled with shame but most of us who suffer with substance use disorders are masters at holding these two perspectives in one mind.

As the steps are worked, our capacity for honesty and compassion will grow. But before the underlying issues of our disease can be addressed - depression, anxiety, trauma, guilt and shame, trouble coping with real life on life's terms, etc. - we need to acknowledge the truth about our situation. We need to find a way to manage our compulsions so that they stop controlling us.

The combination of arrogance paired with self-loathing contributes to denial. Denial is a serious condition that affects both the person with the substance use disorder and their family. It basically means having a messed up perspective on life.

I'm tired of all this - so tired. My bed has been floating forty days and nights on the flood of my tears. My mattress is soaked, soggy with tears. The sockets of my eyes are black holes; nearly blind, I squint and grope.
Psalm 6:6-7 The Message

STEP 1: WE ADMITTED WE WERE POWERLESS OVER OUR DEPENDENCIES AND THAT OUR LIVES WERE UNMANAGEABLE.

Consider Your Story

List the ways your life is unsatisfying to you.

What are you sad about? Mad?

How have you been suffering in ways that you have not wanted to admit? Explain.

Step 1: We admitted we were powerless over our dependencies and that our lives were unmanageable.

Study #7- Step 1

Moment by Moment - Meditation

Practice Centering Prayer. See Appendix A for further guidance.

Prayer for the Moment[3]

> *The people walking in darkness have seen a great light; on those living in the land of the shadow of death a light has dawned.*
> *Isaiah 9:2 NIV*

We know what it is like to walk in darkness. We know what it is like to live in the shadow of death. But we also are beginning to experience what it is like to see. The darkness of denial is giving way to the light of honesty in our lives.

Of course, when you have lived in darkness as long as we have, the light can be painfully bright. We see the truth about ourselves and our self destructive behavior. We see the truth about our refusal of love. We see the truth of our brokenness. We see old pain. We see current behaviors that damage ourselves and others. The light dawns. It is not a pretty sight.

But God does not send light into our darkness to shame us. The exposure may trigger our deep shame, but this is not God's purpose. God's light is like the light of dawn. It is a light that signals that something new is happening. A new beginning is possible. The light that God brings into our dark world is a light of hope.

Recovery is God's light coming into our darkness. The light exposes. We begin to see clearly the ways we have sinned and the ways other people have sinned against us. And the light provides hope. In the light we see the possibility for new beginnings.

---

[3] Prayers for the moment are excerpted with permission from *Rooted in God's Love, Meditations on Biblical Texts for People in Recovery* by Dale and Juanita Ryan, 2005, pp. 26-27.

STEP 1: WE ADMITTED WE WERE POWERLESS OVER OUR DEPENDENCIES AND THAT OUR LIVES WERE UNMANAGEABLE.

Lord, your light hurts my eyes.
It is too bright.
I see too clearly now.
It is too painful for me.
Help me to believe that your light is
not to bring shame
but to bring hope
into my dark world.
Light of Heaven, embrace me with your warmth.
Heal me with your bright rays.
Give me life.
And hope.

Amen

Additional Prayers:

Step 1: We admitted we were powerless over our dependencies and that our lives were unmanageable.

Thoughts for the Day

"Alcoholism is a primary, chronic disease with genetic, psycho-social, and environmental factors influencing its development and manifestations. The disease is often progressive and fatal. It is characterized by continuous or periodic: impaired control over drinking, preoccupation with the drug alcohol, use of alcohol despite adverse consequences, and distortions in thinking, most notably denial...Denial is used here not only in the psychoanalytic sense of a single psychological defense mechanism disavowing the significance of events, but more broadly to include a range of psychological maneuvers designed to reduce awareness of the fact that alcohol use is the cause of an individual's problems rather than a solution to those problems. Denial becomes an integral part of the disease and a major obstacle to recovery."[14]

Take out alcohol and insert a host of other mind-numbing dependencies and the definition still works. Dependencies can include: spending, eating, sex, exercise, dieting, shoes, drugs, fantasy living and more.

"Denial becomes an integral part of the disease and a major obstacle to recovery."

How many times have we heard - "You are in DENIAL! Get your act together!"? Did it help? Did we snap out of it and get our acts together? The problem with this approach is obvious. Denial is such an "integral part of the disease" that asking me (and you) to get our acts together is in itself a sign that our family and friends are also in denial about the pervasive nature of this disease.

Denial is not intentional; it is not lying. It is a symptom that our brain has been hijacked and we are not able to perceive ourselves, others, God and our circumstances with any degree of accuracy. This is not the same as saying we are bad people, or that we are stubborn, or that we are evil. It is saying that our condition has gotten to a stage on the spectrum of disorder that our capacity for clarity is impaired.

How do we get around denial? We make a decision to trust someone other than ourselves. Usually this is a person who can relate to our situation without judgment. The First Step requires acknowledgement: I am suffering from a substance use disorder that is bigger than my ability to think my way out of the problem. I need help. Not just any kind of help - the kind of help that understands how to treat this particular disease!

For troubles without number surround me; my sins have overtaken me, and I cannot see. They are more than the hairs of my head, and my heart fails within me.
Psalm 40:12 NIV

---

[14]This definition was prepared by the Join Committee to Study the Definition and Criteria for the Diagnosis for Alcoholism of the National Council on Alcoholism and Drug Dependence and the American Society of Addiction medicine and was approved by the Board of Directors February 3, 1990 and February 25, 1990 respectively.

STEP 1: WE ADMITTED WE WERE POWERLESS OVER OUR DEPENDENCIES AND THAT OUR LIVES WERE UNMANAGEABLE.

Consider Your Story

Thoroughly list all the unmanageability in your life. Think about your relationships, finances, job status, dreams, living arrangements, etc.

How has denial (a stubborn resistance to living honestly and an intentional pursuit of unreality) impacted your relationships and life circumstances?

Study #8 - Step 1

Moment by Moment - Meditation

Practice Centering Prayer (see Appendix A to review the details). When finished, make a note of the time you were able to sit with the practice. Over time, our capacity to pray in this way grows.

Prayer for the Moment[15]

"I will set out and go back to my father and say to him: 'Father, I have sinned against heaven and against you. I am no longer worthy to be called your son'...But while he was still a long way off, his father saw him and was filled with compassion for him."
Luke 15:18-20

It is difficult to think and feel about ourselves in Godly ways. Many of us think that the prodigal son got it right. He had a well-practiced speech: "I am no longer worthy". How like our speeches to ourselves! If we hear about our unworthiness often enough, especially in childhood, and if we internalize the speech thoroughly, it becomes a part of us. Many of us know this particular speech so well that we can feel unworthy for no particular reason. We do not feel unworthy because of something we have done or said. We feel unworthy because of who we are. Many of us even think that the more unworthy we feel, the more likely the Father will be to welcome us back home!

But the Father responds quite differently from the prodigal's expectations. The Father was "filled with compassion" and he ran to his son and he kissed him. When the prodigal finally got his speech out, the Father did not spend time arguing the point. Instead he honored the son with a robe, a ring and a party. He treated the prodigal in ways designed to build a very different kind of self understanding.

Our goal is to learn to think and feel about ourselves in ways that are consistent with the way God thinks and feels about us. God's perspective is a surprising contrast to our own. God does not join our internal chorus which is so persistent at proclaiming our unworthiness. Instead God says, "You are my child. You are loved!"

---

[15] Prayers for the moment are excerpted with permission from *Rooted in God's Love, Meditations on Biblical Texts for People in Recovery* by Dale and Juanita Ryan, 2005, pp. 102-103.

Lord, I have not
learned to think and feel about myself
in healthy ways.
Teach me to think and feel about myself
in ways that are consistent
with the way you think and feel about me.
Help me to listen when you say
"I love you."
Help me to take it in.

Amen

Additional Prayers:

Thoughts for the Day

Spiritual gurus tell us that the true source of happiness is found when we experience the presence of God. They also report that we all lose the key to happiness along the way, which I suppose is another way of saying that we lose conscious contact with the God of our understanding (more on this in a future Step). Many write about this spiritual malaise as a form of spiritual sleepiness. Some say it is a loss of God-consciousness.

This fascinates me. I did not grow up in a religious home. My maternal grandparents were people of faith and I was blessed to have them expose me to religion during my summer visits. I attended children's Sunday School classes and listened to weekly sermons that seemed way too long. Mostly I remember the crackers were stale but the grape juice was tasty. The church was unairconditioned and my legs stuck to the pews with the glue of sweat and left a pattern on my bare skin from the crinoline that often lined my Sunday-go-to-church outfit custom handmade by my grandmother - including hat, gloves and patent leather shoes. Uncomfortable? Yes. But I enjoyed both the ritual and the way it felt walking into church all dolled up.

My sporadic church exposure to faith in my grandparents' conservative Southern Baptist Church was confusing for a number of reasons. Among the top contenders was learning that the reason for a string of Senior Pastors' mysterious disappearances from the pulpit was not the result of a serial killer. I was eventually told about how each participated (in their own unique way) in a series of pastoral indiscretions which led to their firing, not their burial. That information left me wondering if anyone practiced what was preached.

As a pastor, I have heard many stories of spiritual abuse over the years. No wonder we lose our keys to happiness! It is easy to confuse the presence of God and our experiences with the people in our lives who claim to represent him. I know my community must struggle to find grace and mercy for me when my words do not match my behaviors.

As we go through the steps we will have many opportunities to unpack some of the confusions and abusive practices that have masqueraded as spirituality. If you have been wounded by spiritually abusive practices, consider the possibility that our exposure to religion is not representative of the God whose story is told through the scriptures. It is also possible that even the most well-intended teacher has misinterpreted scripture. We will continue to unpack this as we go through the steps. In the weeks ahead, I invite you to take a fresh look at who God is and how he loves you. If you have experienced spiritual abuse, please talk to someone who can support your journey to healing.

When I kept it all inside, my bones turned to powder, my words became daylong groans. The pressure never let up; all the juices of my life dried up.

Psalm 32:3-4 The Message

Consider Your Story

How has your spirituality impacted your recovery? Journal both the positive and the negative effects of your faith on accessing recovery. Include what concerns you about entering recovery as a person of faith.

What causes you the most pain in your life?

Study #9 - Step 1

Moment by Moment - Meditation

Spend a few minutes breathing in and out. In and out. Notice your breath. If your mind chatters away, just return your attention to your breathing as soon as you notice. After a few minutes, take two deep breaths as you let your troubles go.

Prayer for the Moment[16]

> *Many are saying of me, "God will not deliver him."*
> *But you are a shield around me,*
> *O Lord; you bestow glory on me*
> *and lift up my head.*
> *Psalm 3:2-3*

We receive messages about ourselves from the important people in our lives. We internalize these messages and carry them with us - repeating them to ourselves as if they were gospel truth. When the messages are shaming messages then the internal chorus chants "You are not lovable. You are beyond repair. Even God cannot help you."

This chorus is a chorus of lies. The psalmist rejects these lies. And we need to begin to reject these lies as well.

The Lord is a "shield around me," the psalmist says. A shield protects. It comes between the blows of an enemy and a person's vulnerable places. Most shields are small and can only protect a limited area from attack. But the shield which the Lord provides completely surrounds us. We can let this shield protect us from these attacking messages.

The psalmist also says that the Lord "bestows glory on me and lifts up my head." heavy burdens of shame, neglect and abuse have bowed our heads. The Lord listens, pays attention and cares about us. God's love counters the voices of our internal shame-chorus so that we can lift our heads. God replaces our shame with glory. It is a picture of a ragged, neglected child whose head is bowed and shoulders are bent. A king sees the child and goes to him. The king gently lifts the child's chin until his eyes meet his own smiling eyes. He asks the child to come home and live as royalty with him. The child is loved, honored, protected. You are that child. God lifts your head and bestows glory on you.

---

[16] Prayers for the moment are excerpted with permission from *Rooted in God's Love, Meditations on Biblical Texts for People in Recovery* by Dale and Juanita Ryan, 2005, pp. 104-105.

STEP 1: WE ADMITTED WE WERE POWERLESS OVER OUR DEPENDENCIES AND THAT OUR LIVES WERE UNMANAGEABLE.

God help me to stop listening
to lies about you.
Help me to stop listening
to lies about me.
Bestow glory on me.
Lift up my head.

Amen

Additional Prayers:

Step 1: We admitted we were powerless over our dependencies and that our lives were unmanageable.

Thoughts for the Day

Anyone who experiences a substance use disorder is inevitably confronted with the ways in which their condition robs them of people, places and things they love. Perhaps the greatest loss of all is the way we lose ourselves.

As experts wrestle with the nature of SUD – its causes, impact, and best treatment practices – a growing chorus of voices talk about what happens to us BEFORE we begin using alcohol, drugs, sex, gambling, shopping (what have you) compulsively to cope. One common precursor to SUD is genetic predisposition; another factor is early exposure and easy access to mood altering substances; finally, early trauma, neglect, stress, even head injuries – are all factors in creating a vulnerability to substance abuses of many kinds.

> "This acknowledgement that I have a life and death situation, as bad as it's been it's only going to get worse, that's really on the part of the alcoholic or the addict [to figure out]. I think there's an awful lot of people that go beyond the first step not having done that [admission] and they have very limited results and it does everyone a big disservice because they can then say that the steps don't work for them, but really, they weren't honest."[17]
>
> By the Book

On this journey, as we think about our unmanageable lives, it is easy for others to see how our substance use has been detrimental to our health and wellbeing. For those of us who struggle (often unconsciously with the effects of: trauma, learning disabilities, difficulty focusing and paying attention, depression, anxiety, reluctance to trust others, rebellion against authority, high risk taking behaviors, a sense of loneliness even in a crowd, etc., our using is a survival strategy. <u>Let me repeat that: for many of us, our using is a **survival strategy.**</u> As we enter recovery, we need to acknowledge that this strategy is no longer working for us, if it ever did. Our using is causing more problems than it is solving. This is a difficult acknowledgement but it is hard to proceed in an effective way without admitting this. Everyone I know who has begun with the first step of recovery did so kicking and screaming. Why? Because we are scared, frustrated and embarrassed! Our compulsive using of "whatever" has been a survival skill, not an attempt to upset all the people who love us or a clever strategy for losing jobs and spending the night in lockup.

---

[17] *https://www.nacr.org/center-for-12-step-recovery/by-the-book-doing-the-twelve-steps/by-the-book-step-1* at 14:34-14:45.

Consider Your Story

As you ponder your current situation, can you think of events that were "traumatic"? Trauma shows up in many forms. It does not have to be something big and dramatic that was reported on the local news channel. It can include having family members with SUDs of their own - who were not as attentive to the children as they should have been. It is traumatic to struggle with gender identification issues. Divorce. Loss of a loved one. Bullying. No one can judge what trauma means to another person. Journal about this without filtering yourself. Do not dismiss anything that comes to mind. Do not compare your trauma to another's, this is NOT a contest.

What other factors may have contributed to your decision to use (whatever your compulsive strategies are)?

Study #10 – Step 1

Moment by Moment - Meditation

Today's prayer includes Psalm 139:14. It's included here in several translations. Take time to slowly read each rendition. Notice how you react to this scripture. Ponder its meaning for you. In closing, thank God for these words of promise.

> *I praise you because I am fearfully and wonderfully made;*
> *your works are wonderful,*
> *I know that full well. Psalm 139:14 NIV*

> *Oh yes, you shaped me first inside, then out;*
> *you formed me in my mother's womb.*
> *I thank you, High God—you're breathtaking!*
> *Body and soul, I am marvelously made!*
> *Psalm 139:14 The Message*

> *I give thanks to you that I was marvelously set apart.*
> *Your works are wonderful—I know that very well.*
> *Psalm 139:14 CEB*

> *I will give thanks and praise to You, for I am fearfully and wonderfully made;*
> *Wonderful are Your works,*
> *And my soul knows it very well.*
> *Psalm 139:14 AMP*

Prayer for the Moment[18]

> *I praise you because I am fearfully and wonderfully made; your works are wonderful, I know that full well.*
> *Psalm 139:14 NIV*

We are God's creation. God made us. And what God makes is wonderful!

This may sound pretty obvious, but we probably need to remind ourselves that it is not "everything and everybody except me" that is wonderfully made. It is "everything and everybody *including* me" that is fearfully and wonderfully made by God.

When we have learned to see ourselves as people without value - when we have internalized contempt as the basis for our personal identity - it is difficult to see ourselves as one of God's wonderful works.

But you are one of God's wonderful works. You are precious to God. You are a unique, irreplaceable expression of God's creative love.

It is good to praise God for making us. It is good to see ourselves as a reason for thanksgiving and awe. God made our minds, our emotions, our needs, our bodies, our creativity, our longings, our hopes. God is a marvelous creator who made us wonderfully.

You are one of God's wonderful works. You can praise God that he made you wonderfully.

---

[18] Prayers for the moment are excerpted with permission from *Rooted in God's Love, Meditations on Biblical Texts for People in Recovery* by Dale and Juanita Ryan, 2005, pp. 106- 107.

Step 1: We admitted we were powerless over our dependencies and that our lives were unmanageable.

Thank you,
Creator God,
that you made me
and that all that you make
is wonderful
including me.

Amen

Additional Prayers:

Thoughts for the Day

I wonder if today's meditation and prayer time was a challenge for you. I STILL struggle to believe that I am fearfully and wonderfully made. I SAY that I know full well that God's works are wonderful, but I struggle to believe that my own choices have not ruined the wonderful work that God "supposedly" did when he knit me together in my mother's womb. As part of my recovery I choose daily to practice believing things - including this - that are difficult for me to accept. Daily I return to this passage trusting in something bigger than I can understand, acting on faith that this is true regardless of how I feel. As an act of discipline, I try to order my thoughts, my emotions, and my behavior in response to this belief, not my internal angst.

Some days are better than others in this regard. We do not need a visit from Freud to understand that it took some doing to teach me that I was fearful but not wonderful. I have two young grandchildren that the world and our family have not yet sullied with confusing messages of "not good enough" - they indeed think they are each wonderful. They cry with abandon when they are hungry, fully expecting to be fed. This is part of their God-given survival skill set AND the result of having parents, grandparents, aunts and uncles who have taught them from the moment that they were born that their needs are not a problem. I am under no illusions; this will not remain their reality. Our best efforts will not be enough to keep them from developing their own insecurities and sense of disconnection. This is a sad truth that is heightened for many due to abuse, neglect, trauma and loss. We are uniquely created to understand that we bear the image of God. This knowledge is forgotten, distorted, or lost for most of us as we grow up in a world that prefers comparing and competing over cooperation and compassion.

What happens when we are assaulted with experiences that do not support our wonder-full origins? We survive. We study the world and give it what it demands from us. **We alter our personhood and create a personality that seeks to either fit in, fight or flee the world around us.** This is survival of the fittest and our definition depends on what our environment requires of us. It is NORMAL for us to build a personality, a way of being in the world. It is INEVITABLE that at some point in our lives we will be shocked to discover that we are at war within ourselves, that our lives are unmanageable, and we need help. Recovery requires that we enter a period of reconstruction in response to the destruction that the disease of SUD and a broken world encourage.

Oh yes, you shaped me first inside, then out, you formed me in my mother's womb.
I thank you, High God - you're breathtaking!
Body and soul, I am marvelously made!
Psalm 139:14 The Message

STEP 1: WE ADMITTED WE WERE POWERLESS OVER OUR DEPENDENCIES AND THAT OUR LIVES WERE UNMANAGEABLE.

Consider Your Story

When the passions are aroused in the non-rational part of our nature, they do not allow the intellect to function properly.
Richard Rohr[19]

Recovery will require us to examine our thoughts, feelings, and behaviors. We will need to trust others to help us find our way back to our wonderful selves. Along the way, we will acknowledge and learn how to make amends for all the ways we have disappointed ourselves and hurt others. But for today, we remember.

If someone asked you what was the most wonderful part of you, how would you answer?

In what ways does your life today deny the best parts of who you are?

What has your using cost you?

---

[19] Just This, by Richard Rohr, p. 15.

STEP 1: WE ADMITTED WE WERE POWERLESS OVER OUR DEPENDENCIES AND THAT OUR LIVES WERE UNMANAGEABLE.

Study #11 – Step 1

Moment by Moment – Meditation

Refer back to the notes on Centering Prayer (**Appendix A**) and practice it today.

Prayer for the Moment[20]

Look at the birds of the air; they do not sow or reap or store away in barns, and yet your heavenly Father feeds them. Are you not much more valuable than they?
Matthew 6:26 NIV

Many of us learn early in life that we need to earn our sense of value. For some, value was earned by entertaining people with our clowning acts. For others, value came from taking care of everyone else. And for others, value was derived from achieving success of some kind. But often there is no way to entertain enough, take care enough or achieve enough to meet our needs for approval. No matter how compulsively we entertain or care or work, we still are not able to feel valued. These substitutes do not meet the deepest longings of our heart. In addition we run the risk of becoming compulsively attached to these substitutes because we fear that the sense of value which they offer is our only hope of finding peace.

The longing to experience ourselves as valued is a fundamental human need. The need is really a need to be heard, seen, enjoyed and loved by others for who we *are* rather than for what we *do*. No amount of earned approval can meet this need. We long to know that we have value simply because we exist. This kind of value cannot be earned, it must be received as a gift.

Jesus says to us, "You are valuable. Simply because you are, you are valuable." the birds of the air are God's creatures. God sees them and cares for them. God made them and God enjoys them. They are valuable. You, too, are God's creation, made and known by God. God sees you and cares for you. You are of great value.

As we grow in our awareness that our true value is a gift already given to us by God, we can begin to let go of the tight hold we have on our substitute strategies for achieving worth.

---

[20] Prayers for the moment are excerpted with permission from *Rooted in God's Love, Meditations on Biblical Texts for People in Recovery* by Dale and Juanita Ryan, 2005, pp. 108-109.

Step 1: We admitted we were powerless over our dependencies and that our lives were unmanageable.

Father, you know how attached
I have become to earning my sense of value.
But, I can never seem to work hard enough.
Thank you, Creator God,
for valuing
the birds in the air.
Thank you, Creator God,
for valuing
me.
Help me to receive this good gift from you.
Help me to see myself as valuable in your eyes.

Amen

Additional Prayers:

Thoughts for the Day

We are constructed to be valued and valuable; to have purpose; to love and serve others; to be loved and cared for. This is how we are wired. As we have tried to conform ourselves to cultural, familial and various other expectations, we have crafted a personality to fit our environment. So long as our personality aligns with our core values and we are at peace with the values we profess, all is reasonably good (there are exceptions to this but assume this is true for a minute and keep reading).

When our constructed worldview and personality are at odds with the essence of who we are and how we were created to engage with the world, our life becomes unmanageable. We are at war with the metaphorical DNA of God's design. Entering recovery can serve as a shock to our system, allowing us the time we need to evaluate our situation. Recovery offers us the opportunity to both deconstruct what we despise about ourselves and reconstruct our lives.

...You can readily recall, can't you, how at one time the more you did just what you felt like doing - not caring about others, not caring about God - the worse your life became and the less freedom you had?....As long as you did what you felt like doing, ignoring God, you didn't have to bother with right thinking or right living, or right ANYTHING for that matter. But do you call that a free life? What did you get out of it? Nothing you're proud of now. Where did it get you? A dead end.
Romans 6:19-21 The Message

Personality and life choices are not static. We can pivot, re-evaluate, start anew. We need a path back to God and a way to our truest selves. Each of us has a unique way we experience our world. When we lose our way we need to reclaim a context for understanding ourselves in a way that is authentic and healthy. This will require us to explore and own our worldview. Recovery (working the Twelve Steps, treatment, therapy, spiritual practices, etc.) provides a supportive and structured approach that helps us figure this stuff out.

Consider Your Story

What problems are you anxious about resolving?

What issues cause you to feel self-pity? Jealousy? Frantic?

How do these contribute to your life's unmanageability?

STEP 1: WE ADMITTED WE WERE POWERLESS OVER OUR DEPENDENCIES AND THAT OUR LIVES WERE UNMANAGEABLE.

Study #12 - Step 1

Moment by Moment - Meditation

Spend a few moments in quiet reflection. When the military Special Forces need to find calm in the midst of crisis, they practice tactical breathing. Yoga teachers call this box breathing (according to Brenè Brown in her latest book *Dare to Lead*).[21] For detailed instructions go to **Appendix A**.

Prayer for the Moment[22]

> *...Do not fear, for I have redeemed you; I have summoned you by name; you are mine.*
> *Isaiah 43:1 NIV*

Abandoned. Neglected. Alone. Many of us share these painful struggles. Unfortunately, many of us have struggled with them from very early in life. People from dysfunctional families often feel that they were never acceptable to their parents. Many struggle with the feeling that they can never be good enough to receive attention. If reinforced by rejection or abandonment from friends, colleagues or other significant people in our lives, we can easily conclude that we don't really belong at all.

Humans have a deep longing to belong - to be emotionally bonded with others. Social isolation can be very painful. But social isolation may have felt like the only option available to us as children. Attempts at closeness may have meant experiencing control, abuse, rejection or loss. We may have pulled away to protect ourselves, even though it left us lonely and afraid.

God comes to our lonely, anxious hearts and whispers our name. God says, "I see both the fear you have of closeness and the deep longing you have to belong. I have come to comfort you and to respond to your need. I have been seeking relationship with you. You belong. You belong to me. You are my child."

It may frighten us - this invitation to belong to God - even though we long for it. It may frighten us because we expect pain, disappointment, over-control and rejection. But gradually, as we continue the healing process, we can allow God to meet this deep need. We can allow ourselves to belong more and more to God.

---

[21] Brenè Brown, *Dare to Lead, Brave Work. Tough Conversations. Whole Hearts.* (Vermilion, an imprint of Ebury Publishing, 2018), p. 256.

[22] Prayers for the moment are excerpted with permission from *Rooted in God's Love, Meditations on Biblical Texts for People in Recovery* by Dale and Juanita Ryan, 2005, pp. 110-111.

Step 1: We admitted we were powerless over our dependencies and that our lives were unmanageable.

Help me, God, to allow myself
to belong to you.
Thank you for calling me
by name.
Thank you for saying 'you are mine'.
I want to belong to you, God.
Help me to heal, Great Physician,
so that I can accept
my place in your family.
Take away my fear, Father.
Give me the courage
to belong to you.

Amen

Additional Prayers:

Step 1: We admitted we were powerless over our dependencies and that our lives were unmanageable.

Thoughts for the Day

When my brother entered treatment my parents were less than enthusiastic. Once they learned that a "family weekend" was part of the package they were downright hostile. They attended anyway, dragging their bad attitude along with them like a security blanket. During one particularly tough meeting with a therapist my brother shared his thoughts, feelings and some of his actions. I mainly remember his resentment and rage at all of us for putting him in treatment. He recalls how hard it was to have such big feelings and to share them with a family he no longer trusted.

By the time our family had access to treatment, we had all become adept at wearing masks and playing predictable roles. We all brought secrets into the therapy session and my brother later confessed that he was particularly irritated that only his secrets seemed to be open for discussion. In hindsight, I suspect these various roles helped us cope and enabled us to survive. The chaos and conflict that active addiction caused in our family did not leave much room for creativity, collaboration and addressing the needs and wants of the entire family as they arose. Our rigid roles enabled us to think and feel less. Our roles served as a means of energy conservation so that we had what we needed to fight and fume and blame and berate one another. These common characteristics that plague most families who struggle with SUD allow the disease to flourish.

"Mask" is a Greek word that means *"engraving in a stone"* and that accurately summed up each of my family members. We were stone cold. Furious. Enraged. Embarrassed. Frustrated. Ashamed. And fake. Those who helped us participate in recovery (therapists, sponsors and others) served as sculptors, working to remove the excess of our protective shields and masks to "reveal" the hidden person within. Not everyone was willing to cooperate with the process. Recovery is the spiritual process of chipping away at our defense mechanisms while building up our capacity for honesty, coping, and living out our life's purpose. It is hard intensive work; it is art; it is a sacred journey. This is not unlike the work God promises to do with us, shaping and molding us.

Then God's Message came to me: "Can't I do just as this potter does, people of Israel?" God's Decree!
"Watch this potter. In the same way that this potter works his clay, I work on you..."
Jeremiah 18:5-10 The Message

As I worked my recovery program, I felt conflicted, resistant to this idea of God "working on me". I trusted no one. Including God. But desperate times called for desperate measures and slowly, gradually, I began to trust others to help me. Decades in, I can see how the early masks and armor that my family wore to cope with our family issues contributed to my reluctance to trust and to address my own issues. Sometimes the hardest part of recovery for me is trusting that there are different ways of living than what I learned as a child.

Step 1: We admitted we were powerless over our dependencies and that our lives were unmanageable.

Consider Your Story

What role have you played in your family?   (Common options include: hero, scapegoat, addict/alcoholic, lost child, enabler, mascot/clown.)

What part do you think your family is prepared to play in your recovery?

Journal how you feel about interacting with your family and other loved ones now that you have entered recovery.

How do you feel about God molding and shaping you?

Study #13 - Step 1

Moment by Moment - Meditation

Return to Centering Prayer as a meditation practice today. For details, go to **Appendix A**.

Prayer for the Moment[23]

For we are God's handiwork, created in Christ Jesus to do good works, which God prepared in advance for us to do.
Ephesians 2:10 NIV

God is a very capable craftsman. God's workmanship is of the highest quality. We are God's workmanship. We are the art of a competent Creator.

Notice in this text that our creation "in Christ Jesus" means that we are competent as well. We are like our Creator in that we have been created "to do good works". God who is capable of good works made us to be capable of doing good works as well.

This is quite a contrast to "you can't do anything right". In dysfunctional families and toxic institutions we learn to doubt our competence. This doubt compels us to work harder and harder to demonstrate our abilities. No matter how hard we try, we can't try hard enough. We learn that our problem is not that we are human and occasionally make mistakes but that we are incompetent people. We learn that we are flawed in a most basic way. No matter how compulsively we try, we can't ever get it right.

This text is an affirmation of our competence - of our importance in God's plans. God affirms us by saying "there are good things for you to do, and I believe you can do them". Notice that the text does not say that we need to do good works to earn God's love or to win God's approval or that we have to do the work perfectly or compulsively. What it does say is that God sees each of us as capable of good works. God invites us to participate in the creative, redemptive work that God is doing in the world. God sees us as capable.

---

[23] Prayers for the moment are excerpted with permission from *Rooted in God's Love, Meditations on Biblical Texts for People in Recovery* by Dale and Juanita Ryan, 2005, pp. 112-113.

You are competent, God.
Your works are good works.
It amazes me that you see me as competent.
Thank you for believing in me.
Help me to trust your words of affirmation.
Help me to find joy in doing good.

Amen

Additional Prayers:

Thoughts for the Day

In my family of origin, SUD is as common as the various shades of green eyes that mark us as kin. Although researchers are a long way off from nailing down a specific genetic code that indicates our predisposition for addiction, the genetic component that makes us vulnerable to becoming addicted is a reality that is no longer disputed among researchers (who tend to like to argue about such things).

Our family met the criteria to be labelled an "addictive family system". (I prefer "Compromised Family System" today as a way to combat stigmatization.) Along with a propensity to develop SUDs, we also have all the makings of the disordered family system that accompanies SUD. Each of us occupy specific family roles. Our family was prone to secrets and not open to outside feedback. In my birth family, as a firstborn child, I was predictably considered the family "hero" - always trying to make somebody proud. I tried to be good and compared to my brother with the SUD I performed like a Rock Star. Because I was in this system, however, I would have NEVER thought of myself as good or capable of doing good. Even in my own recovery all these many years later I still struggle to not self-identify as an inadequate person. Families suffer from the same feelings of shame as the family member/s with a substance use disorder. My brother with the SUD eventually told me that during his using he felt a lot of shame. He was shocked when I replied, "Me too."

For whatever reason, families struggling with substance use disorder find it hard to seek treatment. What we are all extremely competent at is blaming ourselves, other family members, the system, etc. Deep down, every family member struggles to believe that God or man finds them acceptable because we are so much better at criticism - of self and others.

As Jesus walked along, he saw someone who had been blind from birth. The disciples asked Jesus,
"Rabbi, was it this individual's sin that caused the blindness, or that of the parents?"
"Neither," answered Jesus. "It wasn't because of anyone's sin - not this person's, nor the parents.
Rather, it was to let God's works shine forth in this person."
John 9:1-3

Let's be clear - God doesn't cause us to stumble so that his light shines brighter (read the book of Romans). But what I believe this passage is teaching us is that blaming is not the way to peace; it is certainly not helpful in recovery. Imperfection is the state of humanity. In the days ahead, working the 12 Steps will provide each of us an opportunity to change the question most often asked in families under duress. Stressed out families ask, "Who's at fault and how do we fix them?" A better question is, **"What help do we need and how do we access it?"**

Consider Your Story

Who and what have you blamed for your current situation?

When have you felt like a prisoner of your own choices? Journal about this experience.

Journal about your loneliness.

Study #14 - Step 1

Moment by Moment - Meditation

Practice the tactical (or box breathing) meditation. Details can be found in Appendix A on pg. 92.

Prayer for the Moment[24]

This then is how we know that we belong to the truth, and how we set our hearts at rest in his presence whenever our hearts condemn us. For God is greater than our hearts, and he knows everything.
1 John 3:19-20

Sometimes it is difficult to believe that we "belong to the truth". Sometimes it is difficult to imagine having our "hearts at rest". The part of our heart that is damaged by shame reminds us of all our inadequacies and failures. As this text puts it: "our hearts condemn us".

In the process of recovery many of us become aware that we have internalized the voice of shame and self-condemnation. We may tell ourselves that we are unlovable. Or, we may tell ourselves that we are worthless. Or we may tell ourselves that we are not capable. These are some of the ways we condemn ourselves. We also may question our faith. We may wonder, as this verse puts it, whether "we belong to the truth". Because of our early experiences of rejection and our current self-condemnation, we find ourselves expecting God to condemn us. As a result we cannot rest in God's presence.

But God is greater than our self-condemning hearts. God knows everything. God knows our history. God knows the wounds in our past. God knows our humanness. God knows our failures. God knows that we need healing.

God is greater than our self-condemning hearts. God knows everything. And God does not condemn us.

---

[24] Prayers for the moment are excerpted with permission from *Rooted in God's Love, Meditations on Biblical Texts for People in Recovery* by Dale and Juanita Ryan, 2005, pp. 114-115.

Step 1: We admitted we were powerless over our dependencies and that our lives were unmanageable.

I long to set my heart at rest, Lord.
I long to rest in your presence.
But my heart is full of self-condemnation.
The voices of shame are loud within me.
I am afraid that you will also condemn me, Lord
I am afraid that you will agree with the shame-voices.
Speak to me today, Lord
Speak more loudly than the voices of shame.
Be greater than my heart.
Shame can only feed on the hidden things, Lord,
but nothing is hid from you.
Be more powerful than the shame, Lord.
Let me find rest today in your love.

Amen

Additional Prayers:

Thoughts for the Day

During the first summer of our marriage my husband severely broke his ankle while playing church softball. The second his foot hit the bag he knew he was in trouble; his foot pointed in the wrong direction and flopped around like a fish out of water as his teammates hauled him off and parked him on the hillside bordering the field. At first, his friends did not want to acknowledge the seriousness of the injury. "Walk it off!" they encouraged. Afraid that they would forfeit the game because of the slim turnout of players that night made Pete invaluable so long as he could play.

Once he was deemed a non-contributor, they left him on the sidelines and continued to play one man down. A wife on the opposing team finally found a pay phone (no cell phones back in those days) and called me to come fetch my now worthless husband. To be fair, when his friends heard that he had been rushed into surgery and told he may never walk normally again they apologized for their competitive ways.

Decades later, I still ponder this story. I marvel at how easily we abandon our core values for our passions. When the scriptures tell us that we belong to the truth, it is in no way implying that we are actually living by the truth. What it is saying is this: God gets us. He is truth. He is greater than our hearts, our passions, even the way other humans talk about him. We can rest in his presence because he is safe, not because we have figured out how to get life right. We can and will make mistakes - this does not change God's attitude toward us.

But there is a caveat. We need to pay attention and acknowledge the truth about ourselves. We need to wrestle when our life is out of sync with what we say we value. On that hot August night in 1979 an entire team of Christian men were so distracted by their softball record that they let a fallen friend lay forgotten in agony while they returned to their respective positions.

Step One challenges us to acknowledge the real deal with ourselves, to name our compulsive way of being in the world AND its devastating effects on our lives (and the lives of others). We do not thrive when our life is unmanageable. The chaos creates a forgetfulness that crowds out love to make room for our addiction. When we are not living a manageable life, we are feeding shame and condemnation. That stuff does a good enough job of bringing us down on its own - it does not need us feeding it more fodder by living unconsciously!

My dear children, let's not just talk about love; let's practice real love. This is the only way we'll know we're living truly, living in God's reality. It's also the way to shut down debilitating self-criticism, even when there is something to it. For God is greater than our worried hearts and knows more about us than we do ourselves.
1 John 3:18-20 The Message

STEP 1: WE ADMITTED WE WERE POWERLESS OVER OUR DEPENDENCIES AND THAT OUR LIVES WERE UNMANAGEABLE.

Consider Your Story

What effect has your unmanageable life had on your relationships?

What do you need to acknowledge today?

What have you needed so badly that it caused you to forget how to love?

STEP 1: WE ADMITTED WE WERE POWERLESS OVER OUR DEPENDENCIES AND THAT OUR LIVES WERE UNMANAGEABLE.

Study #15 - Step 1

Moment by Moment - Meditation

My friend Debi cannot meditate in any of the "traditional" ways she hears her friends talk about. She's too antsy. Sitting quietly triggers her; it inflames her shame. However, she believes in the value of meditation and the research studies that confirm meditation's effectiveness in restoring a brain damaged by Substance Use Disorder. What Debi has found helpful is practicing a "walking meditation". It's just what it sounds like - she walks. She finds it particularly helpful to walk surrounded by nature. But on days when that isn't possible, she simply walks wherever she can. She counts her breaths. She notices the way her body moves; the air on her skin; the beating of her heart. If you find seated meditation difficult, try a walking meditation!

Prayer for the Moment[25]

If we claim to be without sin, we deceive ourselves and the truth is not in us. But if we confess our sins, he is faithful and just to forgive us...
1 John 1:8-9 NIV

Few people will be so overt as to say "I am without sin". Self-deceit is rarely that obvious. It often comes masked in socially acceptable and socially rewarded forms of behavior. Perfectionism, for example, is a common expression of self-deceit. We try very hard to look good. Sometimes we work so hard to look perfect that we nearly convince ourselves that it's true. Then, in the moments when we suddenly remember our human condition, we feel shame and self-contempt. And this often makes us want to work even harder to cover over reality with more layers of self-deceit.

But self-deceit will never lead to change and growth. Only honesty can bring change. Recovery begins as we honestly face our failures, our wrong-doing and our self-destructive choices.

For people who have tried very, very hard to be very, very good, facing reality can be painful work. The courage to pursue taking an honest inventory of our lives is not possible without some source of compassion and forgiveness that can replace our shame and self-contempt. The good news is that God is compassionate and forgiving. God freely, joyfully, completely pardons. Because of this hope, we can look honestly at ourselves. Because we can turn to God and find mercy and pardon, we can make a fearless inventory of our lives.

---

[25] Prayers for the moment are excerpted with permission from *Rooted in God's Love, Meditations on Biblical Texts for People in Recovery* by Dale and Juanita Ryan, 2005, pp. 58- 59.

STEP 1: WE ADMITTED WE WERE POWERLESS OVER OUR DEPENDENCIES AND THAT OUR LIVES WERE UNMANAGEABLE.

> "After attempting it enough times and failing, I guess I came to a point where it was possible for me to ask for help and ask for help from somebody that could actually help me, which is something I sort of had been avoiding for a while.[26]
>
> By the Book

Dear God, I have tried hard.
I have tried harder.
I have tried my hardest.
But it has only led to self-deceit.
Help me, God, I need you.
I need your compassion
to overpower my self-contempt.
I need your forgiveness
to overpower my self-condemnation.
Rid me of self-deceit, God.
And build in me a capacity for honesty.
Not so that I can be perfect,
but so that I can genuinely change.
And, so that I can rejoice
in your love for me.

Amen

Additional Prayers:

---

[26] https://www.nacr.org/center-for-12-step-recovery/by-the-book-doing-the-twelve-steps/by-the-book-step-1 at 7:00.

STEP 1: WE ADMITTED WE WERE POWERLESS OVER OUR DEPENDENCIES AND THAT OUR LIVES WERE UNMANAGEABLE.

Thoughts for the Day

Recovery begins with a single step. A nod of the head. A willingness to try something different. It may come after a moment of clarity; often it is when our backs are to the wall and someone has leveraged their power over us to force us into treatment. Some critics complain about the phrase "we were powerless over", calling it negative and not empowering. It offends their sensibilities.

Here is what I know to be true for me: **it seemed impossible to quit using what my brain thought it needed to survive.** Willpower was ineffective for me when I was struggling with compulsive behaviors that turned into a physiological dependency. This is what powerless means to me. There is something in my life that is so powerful, cunning and baffling that I am unable to comprehend that this thing that I think is making me powerful and in control is actually killing me. IN SPITE OF MUCH EVIDENCE TO THE CONTRARY, I am unable to see the writing on the wall and read its message. At the worst of my using, I was absolutely completely powerless over the denial and self-deceit that served as sentries, blocking the obvious truth that I was dying. Both served at the pleasure of my survival instincts, which were compromised and confused as a result of my eating disorder.

> "I can have all these reasons on this side not to drink, and my one trivial reason over here may be well, I stubbed my toe this morning on the dresser' and that's enough to forget about all this and go for it and there's nothing I can do to stop that. I mean, that's the essence of being powerless.[27]
>
> By the Book

However, none of this made me a powerless person; it did mean I was powerless over the effects my SUD was having on my capacity to reason. Recovery teaches me how to take responsibility for my choices. It has EMPOWERED me by giving me a new, inspired way of seeing God, myself and others. It has provided tools to manage the issues that drove my substance use. It has given me the support I needed as I regained my footing and found my capacity for taking the next right step. For me, it served as an acknowledgement that my willpower and good intentions were not enough to treat what ailed me. If you have the clarity and willingness to work a recovery program because you know you have a problem, that is awesome. But this was not my situation. Investigate your situation. Give your body time to adjust to and withdraw from what holds you hostage. Take the time to learn and heal. Then see if you can agree that your substance use has robbed you of freedom.

For when I am weak, then I am strong.
2 Corinthians 12:10 NIV

---

[27] https://www.nacr.org/center-for-12-step-recovery/by-the-book-doing-the-twelve-steps/by-the-book-step-1 at 6:04.

Consider Your Story

What convinced you to enter treatment?

In what ways are you ambivalent about your need for treatment?

If you were a lawyer and you had to make a case before a judge, what evidence would you present that supports the idea that you need treatment?

STEP 1: *WE ADMITTED WE WERE POWERLESS OVER OUR DEPENDENCIES AND THAT OUR LIVES WERE UNMANAGEABLE.*

Study #16 - Step 1

Moment by Moment - Meditation

Practice breathing and sitting and relaxing your body. Start at your feet and slowly work your way up your body. Notice points of tension. Pay particular attention to your shoulders, neck, jaw and even your hands and feet. Concentrate on breathing into and relaxing each muscle in your body.

Prayer for the Moment[28]

> *So then, let us not be like others, who are asleep, but let us be awake and sober.*
> *1 Thessalonians 5:6 NIV*

The first step toward honesty is to pay attention. In the words of this text, the choices we face are either to sleep or to be alert and self-controlled.

There are days when we would rather sleep. There are days when the emotional numbness of denial seems less painful then the alertness required by recovery. Couldn't we just "let it ride" for a day? Couldn't we just "sleep" for a while?

Sometimes people encourage us to sleep. "Why are you still paying attention to that? It was a long time ago!" Or "Why are you still 'holding on' to that? Just forgive and get it behind you." Wouldn't it be great to get this over with quickly and not have to pay attention to it anymore?

There is a rest, a serenity, that comes from God. But it comes from "alertness" not from "sleep". God's peace is not like the "sleep" in this text. This sleep is denial, it is avoidance, it is distraction, it is pretending, it is death. Being alert means that we allow ourselves to see and hear, to use our senses and mind and heart. It means that we pay attention to what is happening inside of us and around us. The text urges us to be alert, to pay attention. Pay attention, it urges, even if life is painful, even if it is not what we want it to be.

---

[28] Prayers for the moment are excerpted with permission from *Rooted in God's Love, Meditations on Biblical Texts for People in Recovery* by Dale and Juanita Ryan, 2005, pp. 60- 61.

Step 1: We admitted we were powerless over our dependencies and that our lives were unmanageable.

Lord, help me to pay attention today!
Help me not to put my feelings to sleep.
I want to be aware of my thoughts and feelings, Lord.
I want to be able to experience both the pain and joy of life today.
Help me to pay attention.

Amen

Additional Prayers:

STEP 1: WE ADMITTED WE WERE POWERLESS OVER OUR DEPENDENCIES AND THAT OUR LIVES WERE UNMANAGEABLE.

Thoughts for the Day

In Abraham Twerski's book *Addictive Thinking,* he talks about denial and self-deception, both of which feels to me like sleepwalking.

Twerski writes, "I cannot stress enough the importance of realizing that addicts are taken in by their own distorted thinking and that they are its victims. If we fail to understand this, we may feel frustrated or angry in dealing with the addict."[29]

I have felt the frustration that comes when we love someone who continues to ignore the consequences of their actions; I have been the person who has frustrated others with my own commitment to a self-destructive path. When has anger ever motivated lasting change? In my experience, never. Instead of judgment and condemnation, what if we looked for a different way to assess our issues?

Denial is a wall of limitation but it is NOT necessarily helpful to think of it as a defect or character or a shortcoming. It is symptomatic of the disease process. If I am active in my substance use, denial is a factor in my decision-making. Denial is a function of a hijacked brain, not a representation of my character. Denial is dangerous. It keeps us from naming our problem/s, which guarantees that we are not free to find a solution. How do we get out from under this burden of self-deception? We start acknowledging what we can. When we are asked to acknowledge things like powerlessness, unmanageability and name our SUD(s), keep in mind that denial will make this admission difficult.

---

[29] Abraham Twerski, *Addictive Thinking: Understanding Self-Deception* (Hazelden, 1997), p. 13.

STEP 1: WE ADMITTED WE WERE POWERLESS OVER OUR DEPENDENCIES AND THAT OUR LIVES WERE UNMANAGEABLE.

Consider Your Story

Describe the physical symptoms over which you are powerless. (Examples: sexual dysfunction, skin issues, headaches, sleep disorder, eating disorders, cardiovascular issues, etc.)

List foods, medicines, drugs, alcohol – anything you keep ingesting even when it is in your best interest to stop.

What feedback are you receiving that is really hard to hear? List hints from this feedback that can help break down the wall of denial.

STEP 1: WE ADMITTED WE WERE POWERLESS OVER OUR DEPENDENCIES AND THAT OUR LIVES WERE UNMANAGEABLE.

Study #17 - Step 1

Moment by Moment - Meditation

Take a few minutes and practice breathing. It sounds silly to think about practicing breathing, but when we are anxious we forget to breathe and we do not notice our breath. Focus on one thing for which you are grateful today.

Prayer for the Moment[30]

No more lying then. Everyone must tell the truth to his fellow believers because we are all members together in the body of Christ.

Ephesians 4:25

Honesty is essential to recovery. Honesty is essential to intimacy. But honesty is not easy.

We were not created to be isolated, independent creatures. We were created to be interdependent. We need each other. In order for us to be helped by others and to be helpful to others, we need to practice honesty. That means we must learn how to talk to each other about our thoughts and our feelings and our needs. We must learn to talk about our struggles and failures, about our dreams and our successes.

Honesty is the soil in which intimate relationships grow. It creates the possibility of being known and loved for who we really are. But it is also full of risks. If we tell the truth about ourselves, people may not listen. They may not want to know. They may not understand. They may judge and reject. They may dislike us. They may give us simple answers to unanswerable questions. They may repeat what we have said to others.

We hesitate to be honest because we have experienced these things in the past. Our feelings may have been minimized. Our thoughts may have been devalued. Our reality may have been denied. But in order to grow healthy relationships - in order to heal and recover - we need to begin to take risks. Learning honesty will be a process for us. It will not come quickly. But as we practice honesty in relationships we will gradually become more secure in telling the truth.

---

[30] Prayers for the moment are excerpted with permission from *Rooted in God's Love, Meditations on Biblical Texts for People in Recovery* by Dale and Juanita Ryan, 2005, pp. 62-63.

I am tired of lying
when it would be just as easy
To tell the truth.
But I am afraid of honesty, Lord.
It's not as easy as it sounds.
Help me to pursue honesty today.
Help me to be honest with you.
Help me to be honest with myself.
Help me to build a community of faith
where honesty is the norm.
Build in me a capacity for truth.

Amen

Additional Prayers:

Step 1: We admitted we were powerless over our dependencies and that our lives were unmanageable.

Thoughts for the Day

Early in my brother's recovery he asked me to support his recovery by going to meetings. I found a support group for family members of "addicts" as we called them in the olden days. In those meetings I learned about codependency; I knew I qualified as a member of that club. By the time he left treatment and entered aftercare I was actively working on my own addiction issue – an eating disorder. In fact, there were many labels that fit me. But that was not all there was to me, just as the labels placed on you do not adequately and fully describe who you are as a human.

Both my brother and I had to dig deeper, get counseling and continue to work a recovery program to discover and appreciate that many factors came together to create the perfect storm that resulted in the self-destructive choices we were making.

We need at least three things in recovery:

1. We need to acknowledge our dependencies and our unmanageable lives with specifics.

2. We need to figure out how to manage life in a more healthy manner.

3. We need to understand and embrace our potential, our promise and the wider range of possibilities that might lead to a rich and satisfying life.

Step One is the beginning of a journey that may feel terrible, but for me it has become a gift. My prayer for you is that you hang in and see where this journey might lead you.

> *"I don't use alcohol or drugs the way that normal people do. I don't even think about them the way normal people do."[81]*
>
> *By the Book*

---

[31] *https://www.nacr.org/center-for-12-step-recovery/by-the-book-doing-the-twelve-steps/by-the-book-step-1* at 10:30.

Consider Your Story

There is so much more to you than your label. Who else are you? What/who do you love? What are your dreams?

How has your substance use enhanced who you are? Improved your love relationships and your interests? Helped you achieve your dreams?

What has substance use cost you in terms of your personhood, your relationships, your interests and your dreams?

Step 1: We admitted we were powerless over our dependencies and that our lives were unmanageable.

Study #18 - Step 1

Moment by Moment - Meditation

Meditation helps wake us up. Our goal is not to turn our brain off or shut down our thoughts. Meditation is helpful for calming us down, getting in touch with our feelings and thoughts, even our stressors. Today, sit with your eyes open and notice. Notice your environment. See colors. Notice the temperature of the room. Find details. After a few minutes, turn your attention to your body and notice - how is your body feeling? Naming our feelings actually reduces their power over us. As you meditate, see what feelings you can name. This activity alone is calming.

Prayer for the Moment[32]

If only my anguish could be weighed and all my misery be placed on the scales. It would surely outweigh the sand of the seas - no wonder my words have been impetuous.
Job 6:1-3 NIV

When we have lived for a long time by the "don't talk" rule, learning to talk honestly and personally can be a real challenge. Our attempts to move away from self-deceit toward honest self-disclosure may be quite awkward. It's not reasonable to expect ourselves to be gifted at telling the truth when we have practiced deceit for so long. Sometimes our words will seem startling. We will feel our pain, find our voice, and the words and emotions will tumble out raw and uncensored. This text calls these "impetuous" words. Another translation of this text calls them "wild words".

It is not easy to break the silence, to talk about what is real, to tell the truth about what we see and hear, to share what we think and feel, to tell our stories. Breaking the silence is like breaking the sound barrier - sometimes it can be quite loud and it can rattle the walls a little. Or a lot. When our misery feels like it "outweighs the sands of the seas," our emotions are going to be intense and our words will sometimes be wild.

Wild words are part of the journey and should not surprise us. Intense feelings sometimes need strong language in order to find true expression.

---

[32] Prayers for the moment are excerpted with permission from *Rooted in God's Love, Meditations on Biblical Texts for People in Recovery* by Dale and Juanita Ryan, 2005, pp. 64-65.

Step 1: We admitted we were powerless over our dependencies and that our lives were unmanageable.

Lord, I am not accustomed to talking.
I am not gifted at honesty.
I have practiced "don't talk"
for a long time.
And now I need to practice honesty.
Help me to be patient
and accepting of my wild words
even when the wild words frighten me.
Help me to pursue the truth.
Give me the courage I need.
You, Lord, who created the worlds with a word,
give me the words I need.

Amen

"[My work is]...to fully concede to my innermost self that I am an alcoholic, I am a drug addict...but I don't have to really understand what that means.[33]

By the Book

Additional Prayers:

---

[33] https://www.nacr.org/center-for-12-step-recovery/by-the-book-doing-the-twelve-steps/by-the-book-step-1 at 9:53-10:02.

STEP 1: WE ADMITTED WE WERE POWERLESS OVER OUR DEPENDENCIES AND THAT OUR LIVES WERE UNMANAGEABLE.

Thoughts for the Day

In recovery I began to make sense of my choices. This took a long, long time. It was like waking up from a deep but restless sleep. In the early days of the journey I came across the writings of Henri Nouwen. Nouwen was a Dutch Catholic priest, professor, writer and theologian. He wrote a ton of books. His writings wrestled with identity – a subject I was in desperate need of exploring seeing as how I had lost mine somewhere along the way. He says that we get lost in one of three particular ways and get stuck by believing that:

- I am what I have. (SUD told me that all I had/needed were the rituals of my using.)

- I am what I do. (SUD told me that losing weight was my highest value.)

- I am what others think about me. (SUD told me that how I looked determined my worth.)

Nouwen is crystal clear that these habitual ways of seeking approval and purpose are distractions and not ultimately satisfying. He believed that we were called to a higher purpose, a life of love and service to others that teaches us that we are more than our possessions, our work or our reputation. This sounds wonderful but a SUD distorts our understanding of ourselves in ways that are just as destructive as the guy who thinks a Porsche confers status, a fancy job gives one power, or the approval of others equals love.

My eating disorder robbed me of my desire to accomplish, so my world became terribly small and isolated. I lost interest in "having" things, relationships and meaningful work. I shrunk down to the bare bones of a survivalist. My eating disorder stole my strength, so that I could no longer participate in the physical activities I loved. My eating disorder was a cunning thing, stealing my interest in others and my willingness to learn from them. Before ED, I was interested in people; curious about their perspective; open to feedback. All this happened and the only thing I noticed was my value when I stepped on the scale. The smaller the better.

"I think the hardest part of the first step [is to] say I have this obsession, I have this craving, it is getting worse, I can't seem to stop...admitting that as opposed to keeping that inside."[34]

By the Book

---

[34] *https://www.nacr.org/center-for-12-step-recovery/by-the-book-doing-the-twelve-steps/by-the-book-step-1* at 17:30.

Consider Your Story

Frankly, there are all sorts of ways to mess up one's life. Fantasy living and grandiosity is one of them. Sometimes in early recovery we latch onto a new obsession. We might daydream about how we can get a job and spend our money on tangible goods that will bring us status, or hold down a job that will win us approval, or win back the love and approval of those who have expressed their disappointment in us while we were using. These thoughts can tempt us to short circuit our treatment. Today, we face that temptation.

If you decided you wanted to bail on treatment, what story would you tell to convince others that you do not need support for your recovery?

Who do you think would buy your story?

Who would encourage you to stay and do the hard work of recovery? What plan can you devise to help you stay connected to those who understand that recovery takes time?

Study #19 - Step 1

Moment by Moment - Meditation

Take a few minutes to read and ponder this quote:

When health is absent, wisdom cannot reveal itself, art cannot manifest, strength cannot fight, wealth becomes useless, and intelligence cannot be applied.
Herophilus[35]

Prayer for the Moment[36]

How long must I wrestle with my thoughts and every day have sorrow in my heart?
Psalm 13:1-2

Sometimes our spiritual distress is centered on questions about God. Where is God? Why doesn't God help? At other times our spiritual distress is centered on questions about ourselves. What is wrong with me? How come I am still struggling this much?

Doubts about ourselves can be profoundly troubling. We wonder if our faith will survive the struggle. We wonder if our faith is strong enough. Often we feel like spiritual failures. The kind of spirituality we have been taught does not envision "good" Christians as people who wrestle with their thoughts and who are sad everyday. We think of "good" Christians as people who trust God and manage to smile in the midst of any circumstance. When we can't manage to do this, we question our faith and criticize ourselves.

But wrestling with our thoughts and experiencing sorrow day after day is often a part of the recovery process. It is not a sign of failure to engage in this hard work. It is a sign of courage. And it is a sign that our faith is alive and struggling. People of real faith struggle in life. People of real faith are people who wrestle with thoughts and who feel sorrow in their heart.

---

[35] Herophilos/Herophilus, 335-280 BC, was a Greek doctor and teacher who was famous for his work as the first anatomist - systematically performing scientific dissections of human cadavers for the purpose of scientific inquiry.

[36] Prayers for the moment are excerpted with permission from *Rooted in God's Love, Meditations on Biblical Texts for People in Recovery* by Dale and Juanita Ryan, 2005, pp. 74-75.

"I think a lot of people, especially newer people to recovery come into it thinking if heroin is my problem, the absence of heroin is the solution. Then they find that in the absence of heroin they are as bad off and maybe even worse than they are taking the drug.[37]

By the Book

Lord, I get so tired of thought-wrestling.
And I am so weary of heart-sorrow.
How long, Lord?
How long does this wrestling and sorrow go on?
Help me, Lord, not to experience
this struggle as spiritual failure.
Help me to see this hard work
as drawing me closer to you.
Remind me today that you are
with me in all of this.
Remind me today that
you understand.

Amen

Additional Prayers:

[37] https://www.nacr.org/center-for-12-step-recovery/by-the-book-doing-the-twelve-steps/by-the-book-step-1 at 17:00-17:26.

STEP 1: WE ADMITTED WE WERE POWERLESS OVER OUR DEPENDENCIES AND THAT OUR LIVES WERE UNMANAGEABLE.

Thoughts for the Day

Father Thomas Keating, like Henri Nouwen, also wrote about strategies for living. He called his work "a plan for happiness" - which, to be clear, he knew was no real plan at all. His point was that this is how we think, not how life works. He believed that most of us look for happiness in the following ways:

- We believe we need power and control to find happiness.

- We believe we need affection and esteem to find happiness.

- We believe we need security to survive and without it there is no hope for happiness.

Keating would NOT have taken his theory too far. I think he would have agreed that we all need to take responsibility for our life choices, that we are created for loving relationships, and that we need a certain level of security in life to thrive. It is hard to be homeless. It is brutal to be poor and without access to basic life necessities.

But Father Keating challenges us to think about our compulsions, our drives. Taken too far they feed our vulnerabilities to particular falsehoods that hinder our growth. If we cannot find a reasonable way to manage life, we are all vulnerable to developing compulsive ways of thinking, feeling, and behaving that can lead to a dependency of some kind. Many times we become obsessed with chasing happiness.

Scripture gives us a different frame of reference. It offers the promise of a God who is crazy about us and offers dire warnings of how our forgetfulness or misunderstandings about the nature of God, ourselves and others can get us in trouble. Here is a scriptural warning that aligns with the false identity notion of Henri Nouwen and the misguided plan for happiness as described by Father Keating.

Understand that the last days will be dangerous times. People will be selfish and love money. They will be the kind of people who brag and who are proud. They will slander others, and they will be disobedient to their parents. They will be ungrateful, unholy, unloving, contrary, and critical. They will be without self-control and brutal, and they won't love what is good. They will be people who are disloyal, reckless, and conceited. They will love pleasure instead of loving God. They will look like they are religious but deny God's power. Avoid people like this.

2 Timothy 3:1-5

Consider Your Story

When asked by others why you use to the point of negative consequences, how do you respond?

Which of the following "plans" do you resonate with? Pick as many as apply. Explain.

- I define myself by what I have.

- I define myself by what I do.

- I define myself by what others think about me.

- I need power and control in order to feel successful.

- I need affection and esteem in order to be happy.

- I need security to feel content.

How have disappointments and heartbreaks in these areas contributed to your using substances to numb your pain? Conversely, how has using hindered your achievement?

Have you considered that your initial choice to use your substance of preference and your continued use despite negative consequences might be related to past suffering that you have not had the time or help to unpack and heal from? Journal about this.

STEP 1: WE ADMITTED WE WERE POWERLESS OVER OUR DEPENDENCIES AND THAT OUR LIVES WERE UNMANAGEABLE.

Study #20 - Step 1

Moment by Moment - Meditation

Choose your favorite meditative practice and.....practice!!

Prayer for the Moment[38]

> *Can a mother forget the baby at her breast and have no*
> *compassion on the child she has born?*
> *Though she may forget, I will not forget you!*
> *See, I have engraved you on the palms of my hands.*
> *Isaiah 49:15-16*

We may experience abandonment from a spouse who turns away from us to their addiction of choice. We may experience feeling like we have been rejected by friends. We may struggle with memories of parents who were not compassionate with us. Or memories of parents who forgot us in one way or another. Sometimes these experiences are so familiar that we expect them to be part of all our relationships - including our relationship with God.

And so we say to God: "You will abandon and reject and forget me just like all the others!"

God responds to our distress with words of reassurance. We are not always able to take in the reassurance that is offered to us. But there are times when it can feel like a drink of cool water to our parched souls.

God says, "I am not like all the rest. I will not forget you. Even if your parents forgot you, or your spouse turned away, or your friends left, I will not forget you. I have engraved you on the palms of my hand."

It may not be easy for us to comprehend, but it is very clear. God says, "I will not forget you."

---

[38] Prayers for the moment are excerpted with permission from *Rooted in God's Love, Meditations on Biblical Texts for People in Recovery* by Dale and Juanita Ryan, 2005, pp. 80-81.

Step 1: We admitted we were powerless over our dependencies and that our lives were unmanageable.

I need reassurance, Lord.
I want to believe
that you will remember.
But I have been forgotten before.
I know you are not like that.
I know it in my head.
But my heart forgets so easily.
Reassure me today, Lord
of your unfailing love.

Amen

Additional Prayers:

Thoughts for the Day

In their book, *A Spiritual Kindergarten,* Dale and Juanita Ryan take readers on a journey through the 12 Steps. In the introduction, they write:

It is also important to know that the Twelve Steps are not the Twelve Concepts. They are not the Twelve Ideas or the Twelve Truths. They are twelve steps to take, twelve disciplines to practice, twelve activities to do. The focus is on action, not on ideas. You do the steps. If you merely believe the ideas that are found in the Twelve Steps, you cannot expect the desired results.[39]

As a pastor of a recovery church, our community "owns" a question and encourages each other to take right action as a result of the answer. We ask ourselves on a regular basis: **What is the next right step?** We do not inquire much about the future. We try not to ruminate over our past. We focus on the day we are living in.

What is our next right step?

I think this is probably the result of the high percentage of our community who are in recovery. It fits the nature of the recovery process. Dale and Juanita encourage their readers to ask a similar question, **"How can I do this today?"** These two questions are more than enough to get your started on your freedom walk. Our prayers are with you as you wrestle with your next right steps!

> "Basically [the first step is] getting to what is real instead of what should be or what I imagine I should be capable of. I have to get to ground zero, I have to get to what is actually there so it is sort of a process of letting that in."[40]
>
> *By the Book*

---

[39] Dale and Juanita Ryan, *A Spiritual Kindergarten, Christian Perspectives on the Twelve Steps* (Christian Recovery International, PO Box 215, Brea, CA 92822), pp. 3.

[40] *https://www.nacr.org/center-for-12-step-recovery/by-the-book-doing-the-twelve-steps/by-the-book-step-1* at 8:50-9:08.

Consider Your Story

Congratulations! You are at the end of your study sessions for the first step. To complete this step, review your notes and answer the following:

I admit that I am powerless over: (name whatever applies)

My life is unmanageable in the following areas. These issues can be small – "I cannot pay for my own cell phone" [because you have no way to earn a living] or large "I have three outstanding felonies" [my future is in the hands of the courts]. Do your best to make a complete list.

My dependencies include:

Closing Prayer for Step 1

Dear God, I, _____ admit that I am powerless and my life has become unmanageable. I ask for your help in my recovery. Denial has helped me avoid the truth of how my powerlessness and unmanageability has affected myself and others. Despair, shame and my own efforts to control my outcomes have clouded my ability to think clearly and resolve problems. I choose to admit this today. Help me. Amen.

A Word of Encouragement

You absolutely did this thing called the First Step. I hope you pause to celebrate your achievement. Up next? We have a workbook for that too: **Step Two: Coming to Believe.** You can find it on Amazon or grab one through our website @ www.nacr.org.

Step Two sounds deceptively simple: *We came to believe that a power greater than ourselves could restore us to sanity.* For Christians, this step sounds obvious. Of course we believe in a power greater than ourselves! For Christians who have suffered spiritual abuse, or for those who do not believe in the God of the bible, this step might seem downright offensive.

My experience with the 12 Steps took me on a surprising journey of faith that did not always match up with what I was taught in church. This was good news for me because my exposure to faith in church was not particularly healthy. If you are reluctant to consider this concept of "coming to believe", I invite you to pause, suspend your doubts for just a bit, and reconsider. Try the Second Step. You can always reject its precepts and return to your original way of thinking about a higher power! If you are a believer, I would ask you to slow down and not assume that you have this step covered. Take your time; go through the process. See what surprises you!

Again, congratulations on your achievement,

Teresa McBean

Appendix A

Prayer and Meditation

Prayer and meditation are effective tools for assisting men and women in recovery. Here are some of the benefits we can expect when we make a daily practice of prayer and meditation:

- helps manage withdrawal symptoms
- lowers blood pressure and normalizes heart rate
- helps with self-awareness, empathy and finding greater meaning in life
- increases conscious contact with God

In Appendix A we have given you a few options for prayer and meditation time. The key is finding prayer practices that we are willing to actually practice!! Eventually, becoming more open to various forms of meditation is helpful, but the absolute most crucial part of meditation is PRACTICE.

The Serenity Prayer[41]

Full Version:

God, grant me the Serenity
To accept the things I cannot change...
Courage to change the things I can,
And Wisdom to know the difference.
Living one day at a time,
Enjoying one moment at a time,
Accepting hardship as the pathway to peace.
Taking, as He did, this sinful world as it is,
Not as I would have it.
Trusting that He will make all things right
if I surrender to His will.
That I may be reasonably happy in this life,
And supremely happy with Him forever in the next.
Amen.

Short Version:

God, grant me the Serenity
To accept the things I cannot change...
Courage to change the things I can,
And Wisdom to know the difference.

---

[41] Traditionally Reinhold Niebuhr is considered the author of The Serenity Prayer. A dust up about this claim arose; if you are curious, you can read more about this dispute @ https://www.nytimes.com/2008/07/11/us/11prayer.html

The St. Francis Prayer

Lord, make me an instrument of thy peace -

that where there is hatred, I may bring love -

that where there is wrong, I may bring the spirit of forgiveness -

where there is discord, I may bring harmony -

where there is error, I may bring truth -

where there is doubt, I may bring faith -

where there is despair, I may bring hope -

where there are shadows, I may bring light -

where there is sadness, I may bring joy.

Lord, grant that I may seek rather to comfort than to be comforted -

to understand than to be understood -

to love, than to be loved.

For it is by self-forgetting that one finds.

It is by forgiving that one is forgiven.

It is by dying that one awakens to Eternal Life.

The Lord's Prayer

"'Our Father who art in heaven,

hallowed be thy name.

Thy kingdom come,

Thy will be done,

on earth as it is in heaven.

Give us this day our daily bread.

And forgive us our trespasses,

as we forgive those who trespass against us.

And lead us not into temptation,

but deliver us from evil.

For thine is the kingdom, the power

And the glory, for ever and ever."

Amen

STEP 1: WE ADMITTED WE WERE POWERLESS OVER OUR DEPENDENCIES AND THAT OUR LIVES WERE UNMANAGEABLE.

Prayer Prompts

Guidelines for Centering Prayer

(as stated by Thomas Keating, founder of the Contemplative Outreach Network)

1. Choose a sacred word as the symbol of your intention to consent to God's presence and action within.
2. Sitting comfortably and with eyes closed, settle briefly and silently introduce the sacred word as the symbol of your consent to God's presence and action within.
3. When engaged with your thoughts, return ever-so-gently to the sacred word.
4. At the end of the prayer period, remain in silence with eyes closed for a couple of minutes.

Centering Prayer by J. David Muyskens[42]

In Centering Prayer you choose a word, sometimes called a prayer word, sometimes called a sacred word that expresses your desire to be in an intimate relationship with God. This word says you intend to enter that secret room of communion with God. It is not a time for thinking or for words but for presence. Whenever a thought kidnaps you from that intention, you return to that word as a way of letting go of the thought and returning to God.

Ask the Holy Spirit to give you a prayer word that expresses your desire to be with God in faith and love. You may be led to use your most familiar name for God. Some examples may include the following: God, Jesus, Father, Abba, Mother, Lord, Spirit. Jesus' word was Abba. The early church used the name of Jesus when approaching God.

You may be led to choose another word that expresses, for you, your desire to be in communion with God. Such a word could be love, amor, peace, faith, trust, grace, mercy, joy, silence, stillness, calm, open, presence, yes, amen.

Having chosen a sacred word, you use it for the entire period of Centering Prayer. In time one [particular] word will become second nature for you. As the author of *The Cloud of Unknowing* said, your sacred word becomes attached to your heart.

In the years I have practiced Centering Prayer, I have had only two prayer words. First I used the word Spirit as a familiar name for God. Later I changed to Presence, which symbolizes my consent to the presence of the Trinity and of my being present. I have thought about changing it again, but this word has become so much a part of my subconscious it keeps coming back. It is not a matter of thinking about the word and what it means but using it as a way to free me from all thoughts. A simple, short word works best. Avoid anything complicated or a word that has so many connotations that it will take you into more tangents of thought. At times I do not need the word. I let go of it. Just a gentle turning to God is enough.

---

[42] This article and other great materials on centering pray can be found at: https://www.uppperroom.org/resources/centering-prayer. From *Forty Days to a Closer Walk with God* by J. David Muyskens. Copyright © 2006 by J. David Muyskens. Published by Upper Room Books.

Prayer Practice

Use a sacred word you have already chosen or take a little time to ask the Holy Spirit to give you the prayer word for your Centering Prayer time. Let the word emerge from deep within you as you wait on the Spirit's prompting. Gently introduce that word as you begin twenty minutes of Centering Prayer. With that one word you state your intention to consent to God's presence and action. When you find yourself thinking about something, let go of that thought by returning to your sacred word. This is not a violent or forced action but a very gentle one. Don't change the prayer word during the course of the practice. Close the twenty minutes with thanksgiving.

Guidelines for tactical breathing/box breathing

Box breathing is a simple technique that a person can do anywhere, including at a work desk or in a cafe. Before starting, people should sit with their back supported in a comfortable chair and their feet on the floor.

1. Close your eyes. Breathe in through your nose while counting to four slowly. Feel the air enter your lungs.
2. Hold your breath inside while counting slowly to four. Try not to clamp your mouth or nose shut. Simply avoid inhaling or exhaling for 4 seconds.
3. Begin to slowly exhale for 4 seconds.
4. Repeat steps 1 to 3 at least three times. Ideally, repeat the three steps for 4 minutes, or until calm returns.

If someone finds the technique challenging to begin with, they can try counting to three instead of four. Once someone is used to the technique, they may choose to count to five or six. These instructions plus other tips for healing living can be found at:
https://www.medicalnewstoday.com/articles/321805.php

STEP 1: WE ADMITTED WE WERE POWERLESS OVER OUR DEPENDENCIES AND THAT OUR LIVES WERE UNMANAGEABLE.

Appendix B

Dr. James Morrison[43] helps summarize the medical meaning of addiction. Here are some salient points from his analysis of the subject:

The DSM-5 approach to defining substance use disorder as a core behavior specify that addiction includes behavior, physiological and cognitive symptoms. These problems include –

> a. Problem use. Although it may have once served as a coping mechanism, the use itself is now a problem for the user as well as family and associates.
> b. Pattern of use. It is predictable and habitual.
> c. The effects are significant. In other words, bad stuff is happening as a result of use and is causing problems that have come to the attention of law enforcement, the medical community, at work, among friends and with family.
> d. Distress or impairment to the degree that it interferes with daily living.
> e. Distress is defined as having at least 2 of these 11 symptoms: more use than intended, unsuccessful attempts to reduce use, a lot of time spent getting or using, shirking obligations, social problems, reduced activities, ignoring physical danger of use, use even when physical or psychological problems arise, tolerance, and withdrawal symptoms.

Nearly half of all adult Americans will have a problem with alcohol at some point in their life. Ten percent meet the criteria above. Alcoholism is extremely common. Men are at higher risk than women. There is a heritable component. It has a high occurrence of comorbidities, especially mood disorders and antisocial personality disorder.

Withdrawal symptoms develop when supply is diminished or cut off. Although symptoms vary depending on the substance of choice, the most common include:

- Anxiety, irritability and depression
- Restlessness and immobility
- Sleep disturbance (insomnia or hypersomnia)
- Fatigue, changes in appetite and other physical problems
- Hallucinations

---

[43] Morrison Dr. James, *DSM-5 Made Easy, The Clinician's Guide to Diagnosis*, (The Guilford Press, 72 Spring Street, New York, NY 10012, 2014), pp. 396-402.

Appendix C

The Twelve Steps[44]

Step 1: We admitted we were powerless over our dependencies and that our lives had become unmanageable.

Step 2: We came to believe that a Power greater than ourselves could restore us to sanity.

Step 3: We made a decision to turn our will and our lives over to the care of God as we understood Him.

Step 4: We made a searching and fearless moral inventory of ourselves.

Step 5: We admitted to God, to ourselves, and to another human being the exact nature of our wrongs.

Step 6: We were entirely ready to have God remove all these defects of character.

Step 7: We humbly asked Him to remove our shortcomings.

Step 8: We made a list of all persons we had harmed, and became willing to make amends to them all.

Step 9: We made direct amends to such people wherever possible, except when to do so would injure them or others.

Step 10: We continued to take personal inventory and when we were wrong promptly admitted it.

Step 11: We sought through prayer and meditation to improve our conscious contact with God as we understood Him, praying only for knowledge of His will for us and the power to carry that out.

Step 12: Having had a spiritual awakening as the result of these Steps, we tried to carry this message to alcoholics, and to practice these principles in all our affairs.

---

[44] The original 12 steps are found in "Twelve Steps and Twelve Traditions" page 15, Copyright © 1952, 1953, 1981 by A.A. World Services ®, Inc. All rights reserved. These steps have been modified so as to use more inclusive and communal language.

Step 1: We admitted we were powerless over our dependencies and that our lives were unmanageable.

Made in the USA
Columbia, SC
25 August 2019